The Oregon Trail

A PHOTOGRAPHIC
JOURNEY

Bill & Jan Moeller

2001
MOUNTAIN PRESS PUBLISHING COMPANY
Missoula, Montana

Library of Congress Cataloging-in-Publication Data

Moeller, Bill, 1930-
   The Oregon Trail : a photographic journey / Bill and Jan Moeller.
      p. cm.
Includes bibliographical references and index.
   ISBN 0-87842-442-3 (alk. paper)
   1. Oregon National Historic Trail—Pictorial works. 2. West (U.S.)—
Pictorial works. 3. Oregon National Historic Trail—History. 4. West
(U.S.)—History—1848-1860. 5. Frontier and pioneer life—Oregon
National Historic Trail. 6. Overland journeys to the Pacific. I. Moeller,
Jan, 1930- II. Title.
   F597 .M73 2001
   978'.02'0222—dc21
                                                          2001003189

PRINTED IN HONG KONG BY MANTEC PRODUCTION COMPANY

Mountain Press Publishing Company
P. O. Box 2399 • Missoula, MT 59806
(406) 728-1900

For Bonnie ⁓
we truly could not have done it without her

And for Don ⁓
who is always unfailingly enthusiastic about our work

Contents

Acknowledgments

So many people helped us with this book in ways large and small, sometimes knowingly, sometimes not. To them all, we owe our thanks.

When this project was germinating in our minds, Nancy Wilson, curator of the McLoughlin House in Oregon City, was the first one who encouraged us to go ahead. She steered us in many helpful directions, including to Joleen P. Jensen at the Oregon Historical Society, who provided us with much needed data.

This book depicts the Oregon Trail from east to west; in that same order, here are those who provided us with assistance and information:

In Nebraska: Wayne Brandt and his staff, especially Todd Brauch, at Rock Creek Station State Historical Park; Estaline Carpenter and Lester Jones of the Jefferson County Historical Society; Eugene Hunt, superintendent, Fort Kearny State Historical Park; Steve Scheinost for his information regarding California Hill; Dennis Shimmin, superintendent, Ash Hollow State Historical Park; Jerry Banta, superintendent, and the staff at Scotts Bluff National Monument, who tirelessly answered all our many questions; Mert Davis was barraged with most of the thorny ones and never failed to come up with the answers.

In Wyoming: At Fort Laramie National Historic Site, superintendent Gary K. Howe allowed us to roam freely through his domain after providing us with much valuable information and ranger David Junk directed us to several locations. Also Wayne Grannan, superintendent, Ayres Natural Bridge; Professor Dennis H. Knight, University of Wyoming; Michael A. Massie, curator of South Pass City State Historic Site; Craig Bromley at the Bureau of Land Management in Lander; and Corky Ramsey.

In Idaho: G. A. Brower at Fort Hall and Leonard Carlson, head of the City of Pocatello Parks and Recreation Department; Max Newlin, manager, Massacre Rocks State Park; Eric Bergoch, Twin Falls, Idaho; and Charlie McNeil, Bruneau Dunes State Park.

In Oregon: Bob and Bertha Rennells took us over sections of the Oregon Trail and imparted to us a little of their extensive knowledge about the trail; Robert C. Amdor, superintendent, Whitman Mission National Historic Site; Frank Dixon at the Barlow National Forest ranger station; Sergeant Dan E. Wolf, State Police at Government Camp; Ida Darr; the staff at the Zigzag National Forest ranger station;

Dr. Stephen Dow Beckham, without whose help we may not have had such precise information about Laurel Hill; and Milton W. Belsher, who added to our Laurel Hill knowledge.

To obtain the photographs for this book, we often had to leave established roads and highways and venture onto private land. Permission to do so was never refused. Most of the landowners allowed us free access to their lands and more than a few took the time to show us the trace of the Oregon Trail on their property. (We also learned a lot from them about barbed wire, bulls, rattlesnakes, and gate latches.) These helpful people are: Mrs. Stella Hammett; Ivor Dilky; Steve Lauer; Marion Dehning; Hubert Beal, who made us feel closer to the Oregon Trail because his grandfather had traveled over part of it; Vivian and Vern Kallsen; Jolene Kaufman; John and Albert Meyer; Jack Corbett; and Marvin Fager and his grandchildren, Travis and Robin, who showed us some revealing aerial photographs.

We are especially indebted to Mr. and Mrs. Bernard Sun, who provided not only hospitality, but also a privileged look at artifacts pertaining to the Oregon Trail.

Because we were on the trail for more than six months, we had to depend on a photographic lab that would work with us by mail so we could get our processing done as the film was shot. White's Color Center, Inc. in Omaha, Nebraska, provided us with this most important service.

After our journey over the trail, we completed our research at the Oregon Historical Society with the able assistance of manuscripts librarian Layne Woolschlager, Peggy Haines, and other members of the cooperative staff.

In the states the Oregon Trail passes through, state and local agency personnel have done some fine work in preserving and interpreting the Oregon Trail. We appreciate all their efforts, especially what has been accomplished under the direction of Eugene T. Mahoney, director of the Nebraska Game and Parks Commission.

We are glad that Greg Franzwa compiled his two excellent books, *The Oregon Trail Revisited* and *Maps of the Oregon Trail*. They made following the trail easy and enjoyable.

Permission to use excerpts from certain emigrants' writings was kindly granted by the following institutions and individuals: Baker County Public Library, Baker City, Oregon; The Bancroft Library, University of California, Berkeley; the Neinecke Rare Book and Manuscript Library, Yale University, New Haven, Connecticut; Chicago Historical Society, Chicago, Illinois; The Arthur H. Clark Company, Glendale, California; Mrs. Helen Stratton Felker, Tacoma, Washington; Lane County Historical Society, Eugene, Oregon; the *Signal-American*, Weiser, Idaho; and the *Utah Historical Quarterly*, Salt Lake City, Utah.

Notes to the Reader

Though miles and miles of the Oregon Trail have been plowed under, torn up, and paved over, much of the old trail remains and can be seen today. To obtain the photographs for this book, we followed the Oregon Trail as the emigrants did, beginning in Independence, Missouri, in the spring. We traveled through Kansas, Nebraska, Wyoming, and Idaho, arriving in the Willamette Valley in Oregon in the fall. The emigrants averaged about fifteen miles a day, but our average was somewhat slower. Our idea was to take you, the reader, on a photographic journey along the Oregon Trail so that you can see it in the same order and during the same seasons as did the pioneers who traversed it in the years from 1841 to 1860.

In keeping with the emigrant's point of view, we photographed the trail and its landmarks in areas that are virtually unchanged from yesteryear. To accomplish this, we had to omit some important places, where civilization has encroached too much. As a result, some pertinent locations are missing, including Independence, Missouri, where the Oregon Trail begins. Independence Square today is a charming place in a delightful town, but it is nothing like it was in the days of the Oregon Trail.

Most of the photographs are accompanied by a quote from an emigrant's journal that describes the scene as he or she saw it. (We have taken the liberty of correcting some of the spellings.) Sometimes the emigrant writes about a rushing, tumbling river, and the photograph shows a placid body of water. This is because dams have tamed nearly all these formerly free-running streams. The South Platte River is much narrower—by a mile or more—than it was in the mid-nineteenth century. The Soda Springs in Idaho and the American Falls on the Snake River are now completely submerged under a reservoir. Erosion, too, has taken its toll. Where an emigrant may have described a steep descent may now be a deeply worn, impassable gully.

The pioneers tended to overestimate heights. One early traveler reckoned the Wind River Mountains to have peaks over 20,000 feet high; the highest peak in the range is less than 14,000 feet. Another diarist calculated a place on the Snake River chasm to be a mile deep—considerably more than its actual depth of 400 feet.

The only original man-made structures along the Oregon Trail that we photographed are the Hollenberg Ranch House near Hanover, Kansas, and some of the buildings at Fort

Laramie, Wyoming. All other buildings included are reconstructions. Most of these were rebuilt on the site of the original, but Fort Hall was relocated to Pocatello, Idaho, several miles south of its original location on the Snake River.

Whenever possible, we have included actual Oregon Trail ruts and swales in the photographs; wherever a distinct path or road appears, it *is* the Oregon Trail. Some sections of the trail are now part of ranch roads, but they still follow the trace of the original trail. The ruts may show up as parallel or converging lines of contrasting vegetation. The plant growth in the ruts may be lighter, darker, shorter, or taller than the surrounding growth. Sometimes the ruts appear as fuzzy-edged, straight, black, or gray lines. Often there is nothing more than a depression in the earth. All photographs showing trail ruts have an asterisk (*) at the end of the caption.

To help locate the trail, we use the names of the present-day states in the text, and the maps show the modern borders of these states, even though they did not exist during the years the trail was in use—except for Missouri and Iowa, which became states in 1821 and 1846, respectively. Other modern markers on the maps are towns and major highways.

Should this book whet your appetite for making your own investigation of the Oregon Trail, you'll find it easy to do. Many of today's major highways follow the trail route. At significant sites along the way, you will find historic markers and interpretive displays. Some city, county, and state parks have been established to preserve parts of the Oregon Trail. In localities that have an association with the trail, the visitor center or the chamber of commerce office can provide you with information, maps, and brochures about the trail. You will find a list of sites of interest at the end of this book.

For serious trail following, we highly recommend two extremely helpful books: *The Oregon Trail Revisited* and *Maps of the Oregon Trail*, both by Gregory M. Franzwa and published by Patrice Press. *The Oregon Trail Revisited* includes detailed directions for following nearly every one of the trail's miles, from Independence, Missouri, to Oregon City, Oregon. Another handy book, also from Patrice Press, is *Historic Sites Along the Oregon Trail* by Aubrey L. Haines. It lists, locates, and describes every site connected with the Oregon Trail.

If you want to see the Oregon Trail, don't delay. The great landmarks, such as Scotts Bluff and Independence Rock, will probably always be there, but in some places, remnants of the trail—ruts and swales—are in danger of destruction by man or nature.

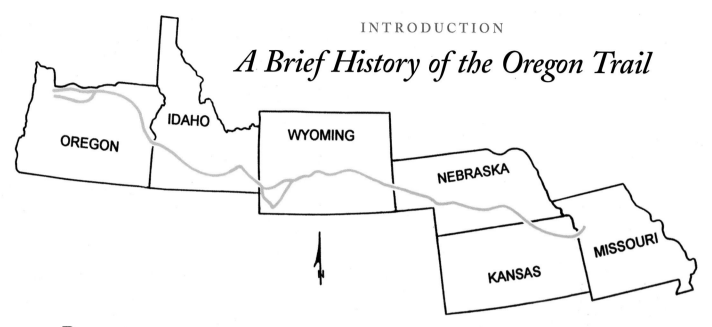

A Brief History of the Oregon Trail

Between 1841 and 1860, tens of thousands of pioneers came over the Oregon Trail—the greatest migration in recorded history—leaving their mark forever imprinted on the face of the land. No single reason explains this vast westward movement; a variety of motives contributed to it.

In the mid-nineteenth century, the West was a new and challenging frontier. The states of Illinois, Indiana, Missouri, Kentucky, and Tennessee had experienced two- and threefold population increases since their settlement, and many of the people living there began to feel hemmed in by neighbors living a mile or two away. Some believed that Oregon would offer them a better life, a place where they could make their fortune. For others, the promise of adventure was incentive enough to move west.

The pioneering instinct, ingrained in so many Americans, drove them to expand the known frontier. Their parents and grandparents were pioneers before them, and they simply carried on the tradition.

Pure and simple patriotism motivated a great many who joined the Oregon movement. The Oregon Territory, which extended from the Rocky Mountains to the Pacific Ocean, belonged jointly to the United States and Great Britain. By virtue of the British Hudson's Bay Company's posts throughout the Northwest, England dominated the region economically. In an effort to claim the territory peaceably, the United States encouraged its citizens to settle there, appealing to their sense of nationalism as well as offering incentives in the form of land subsidies.

1

The first white men who followed the trail west were fur trappers using established Indian trails. In 1812 one of those trappers, Robert Stuart, found a way across the Continental Divide easy enough for wagons to travel over: South Pass in present Wyoming. Even so, it was not until 1830 that wheeled vehicles were taken over this pass. In 1836 a small party led by Dr. Marcus Whitman, a physician and missionary, successfully completed the journey to what is now Walla Walla, Washington. Other missionaries, both Catholic and Protestant, followed. In 1842 the first group of settlers—112 people—headed west from Independence, Missouri. After that, there was no holding back the migrating tide.

During the eighteen-year period of migration over the Oregon and California Trails and the Mormon Trail to Utah, nearly 300,000 people, with some 75,000 wagons and uncountable livestock, coursed over the various routes and left an unmistakable road—as well defined as any modern highway. In many places the tracks are clearly visible today.

Destinations

Although some of the overlanders followed the Oregon Trail only to where the main California

Trail branched off in what is now Idaho, many of them were bound for the Willamette Valley in Oregon, an incredibly fertile plain running in a north-south direction for nearly one hundred miles. They had heard that it was sheltered from violent weather by the Coast Range to the west and the Cascade Mountains to the east. The valley had been heralded as having little snow and a mild climate with no temperature extremes in either winter or summer. Though it rained copiously, there were no severe thunderstorms, hurricanes, or tornadoes. In short, Oregon was ideal for raising crops and appealed to the mostly agrarian emigrants. To reach this promised land, however, one had to traverse vast, treeless plains and deserts, ford rivers and streams, cross mountains, and endure freezing cold and scorching heat.

Departure Points

Independence, Missouri, became the initial departure point for the Oregon Trail because it was the beginning of the Santa Fe Trail, a trade route that had been in use since 1823. Leaving from Independence, the emigrants could follow a well-defined trail for about forty miles, until the Santa Fe Trail branched off to the south.

Most early emigrants arrived in Independence after traveling up the Missouri River by steamboat from St. Louis. They needed teams, wagons, and supplies before they could start their journey. It was not long before enterprising individuals recognized that there was a good deal of money to be made from outfitting the overlanders. Suppliers soon set up shop in St. Joseph, Missouri, advertising that it was the best place from which to leave. Farther north and west than Independence, it eliminated twenty miles and several river crossings from the trip.

Within a few years, wagon trains were departing from several towns along the Missouri River between St. Joseph and Council Bluffs (then called Kanesville), Iowa. The more northern points of departure appealed to would-be pioneers from Illinois and Indiana. They were close enough that they could outfit themselves in their hometowns, buying supplies and equipment from merchants they knew. This spared them from dealing with unethical traders who were apt to gouge greenhorns.

Emigrants leaving from any point south of Council Bluffs followed the south side of the Platte River until they crossed it in western Nebraska. Those who departed from Council Bluffs—by 1850 they were in the majority—stayed on the north side of the Platte. The two trails joined at Fort Laramie, Wyoming, or a little farther west.

A timely departure was crucial for the well-being of humans and animals. The overlanders could not leave too early in the spring because grass for the animals had not yet grown. But they could not delay too long, or the livestock of earlier trains would have eaten all the forage. Furthermore, if they left too late, it would be well into autumn or early winter when they reached the Blue Mountains in eastern Oregon, and they would have to cross the mountains in the snow, if they could cross at all.

The Wagon Train

For security and defense, the emigrants traveled in trains made up of many wagons. Often a train was composed of families that had come from the same area, but companies were also formed of people who had no previous acquaintance with one another. No matter who was in the train, some people would eventually split from the group and join one that did things more to their liking. The cause of much dissension was whether or not to stop to observe the Sabbath.

At a wagon train's departure, or shortly thereafter, a captain was chosen. He made decisions regarding the security of the train, selected where and when to camp, appointed scouts and night watches, and mediated disputes. The job could never be considered permanent: if other members of the train disagreed with the captain, which they did with regularity, he was voted out and replaced with another.

In some cases, the members of a train hired a guide, often a mountain man who was heading west anyway. He knew the route, at least as far as the Rocky Mountains, he had knowledge about the Indians and how they should be handled, and he was invariably a better shot than any of the overlanders and so would be able to supplement their diet with game.

The Routes

The Oregon, California, and Mormon Trails were one and the same until they branched off hundreds of miles west. The Mormons were bound for the fertile lands around the Great Salt Lake, and the Mormon Trail angled southwest at Fort Bridger, near the present-day Wyoming-Utah border. The California Trail branched off at two places in Idaho. The first branch, known as the Hudspeth Cutoff, started at Soda Springs. The other, at the Raft River, became the main trail to California.

Over the years, several shortcuts came into and went out of favor. One of the most popular was the Sublette Cutoff in Wyoming, which lopped a hundred miles off the main trail by heading straight across the Little Colorado Desert to the Green River. The Barlow Road in Oregon, while not a shortcut, was an overland route many of the emigrants opted for to avoid the hazardous water passage down the Columbia River. At certain points, all pioneers, or the guides they hired to lead them, had to weigh whether it would be better to stay on the main trail or to take a shortcut or branch trail. No matter which route they took, there were drawbacks. They might have to ford dangerous rivers, negotiate steep hills, cross desert wastelands, or travel through choking dust.

Wagons and Teams

Most pioneers started out with brightly painted wagons. The sparkling white covers over the wagon boxes were emblazoned with the owners' names, where they were from, and such slogans as: "On to Oregon" and "Oregon or

Bust." The American flag was prominently displayed on many wagons.

The heavy Conestoga wagon, often favored in the East for freighting, was not used on the trail in any great number. The wear and tear on draft animals had to be considered—the supplies were heavy enough without using a wagon that added to the burden. Guidebooks gave specifications for building a suitable wagon and outfitting it.

The versatile covered wagon was ideal for overland travel and made a comfortable, cozy home. The canvas cover was double thickness, the outer shell waterproofed with paint or oil. Storage chests were often built to fit snugly inside the wagon box; others were lashed to the outside. The emigrants arranged extra storage space by building a false floor in the box and sewing pockets onto the inside of the cover.

To keep weight down, iron was used sparingly. Only the wheels and wagon reinforcements were made of iron. Because the big wheels extended well above the floor of the box, the wagons could not turn easily. The lack of maneuverability was considered a small sacrifice, however, because wagons with large wheels were much easier to pull.

Since the wagons had no springs, most people preferred to walk or ride a horse, if they had one, rather than endure the constant jolting and lurching of the wagon. Even the team driver walked, moving alongside the plodding animals, using a whip and spoken commands— and curses—to guide them. The usual rate of travel was about two miles an hour—fifteen miles on an average day—an easy pace for both man and beast.

Oxen or mules were the preferred draft animals. The argument over which of the two was better was never resolved. Cost often determined the choice: mules were three times the price of oxen.

The pioneers became quite attached to their animals, who served them well for hundreds of miles. Man and beast suffered together through heat, dust, and waterless, grassless stretches. When a weary animal lay down in its tracks, it was heart wrenching for its owner to try to coax it to stand and resume its killing work. The sadness when an animal died was exceeded only by the grief of losing a human loved one on the trail.

Wagon Handling

The weight and awkwardness of the wagons made them a challenge to handle on difficult terrain. The emigrants used several techniques to move wagons down hills safely. If the incline was not too steep, the oxen could be left hitched to the wagon to check its speed. Often the wagon's wheels were locked to further slow it. In steeper areas, if there were trees, a rope was tied from the wagon to a sturdy trunk and wrapped around a few times; this served as a snubbing winch to slow the descent. If no trees were handy, every available person was expected to lend a hand at the ropes.

On the steepest hills, if timber was readily available, trees were tied, top foremost, to the back of the wagon as a drag. Usually the branches were cut close to the trunk so their short stubs would dig into the earth. If the top-heavy wagons were to be taken across a steep slope instead of straight down it, ropes were secured to the upper side of the wagon and handlers would keep a strain on the ropes as they walked alongside to prevent it from toppling over.

For fording rivers, the methods were even more ingenious. Wagons had rather high clearance, so crossing shallow water usually presented no problem. But when the depth reached about four feet, to keep the wagon contents dry, the emigrants often raised the wagon boxes by putting blocks on the axles. Some emigrants simply caulked their wagon boxes, making them watertight, and floated them over.

To cross deep water, eight or more teams were hitched to one wagon. In this way, at least one of the teams would always be on solid ground, providing some degree of control over the teams that were swimming. Men would sometimes swim or ride a horse across to scout unfamiliar fords. They often fastened a rope to trees on each side of the river. The rope served not only as a guide for crossing, but helped to prevent swimming animals from being swept away by the current.

Trail Conditions

Whenever they departed, whatever the year, emigrants had to contend with violent prairie thunderstorms that pelted them with drenching rain and hail, and winds that demolished wagons and tents. In early spring, it was often numbingly cold as well as damp. In wet years, swollen streams and rivers became unfordable, causing delays of many days. One wagon train was held up for seventeen days before it could cross a normally insignificant, but at the time heavily flooded, stream.

The desert, which the overlanders reached in midsummer, had its share of problems. The emigrants' discomfort from the heat was heightened by the omnipresent dust of Wyoming, Idaho, and eastern Oregon. The heavy wagon

traffic ground the earth into a fine powder that crept into every crevice, shrouding the wagons, people, and animals.

Past Fort Hall in Idaho, the dust was as bad as, or worse than, any other place on the Oregon Trail. Many accounts tell of driving hub-deep in the stuff—and most wagon wheels were five feet in diameter. At times, the dust was so thick, emigrants walking alongside their wagon could not see their lead team.

During the migration years, the climate was generally colder than it is now. Nearly every wagon train encountered several inches of snow on the ground at South Pass in midsummer. Emigrant journals often tell of chopping ice from ponds and water buckets in late spring and early autumn, where the elevation was not high enough in itself to account for this phenomenon. Whether the emigrants were on schedule or not, they usually experienced snow and cold weather in the Blue Mountains and at the higher elevations on the Barlow Road through the Cascade Mountains.

In addition to the weather, vegetation played a role in the emigrants' comfort. Trees were common in Missouri, and the overlanders regularly encountered stands of timber to provide shade and wood for fuel and wagon repairs until they reached the Platte River. From here on, there was little timber—except in river valleys—until the trail reached the Blue Mountains.

While grass was abundant on the prairies, providing forage for both the buffalo herds and the emigrants' livestock, farther west the trail went through sagebrush country for hundreds and hundreds of miles. As one emigrant wrote: "The everlasting sage seems to have taken full possession of the country." And another said: "Hundreds and thousands of acres with no vestige of anything but this hateful weed."

The Weight Problem

No matter how carefully they planned, the emigrants found that soon after starting out they had to lighten their load. Even on level prairie, the weight of a fully loaded wagon was often too much for the teams to pull or would cause the wagon axles to snap. Later, when the trail began to climb through higher and more difficult terrain, the wagons had to be lightened even more. The process continued far into Oregon. When a team was too weak to pull the wagon, or when the wagon broke down and repairs could not be made, the wagon itself was abandoned.

Everything that was discarded was either burned for firewood or left alongside the trail. The overlanders could not sell things or give them away because everyone on the trail was faced with the same problem. Along one stretch, a traveler wrote of seeing thousands of dollars' worth of furniture, stoves, and equipment heaped up on each side of the trail, appearing like a much-elongated, well-stocked general store. Cast-iron stoves were usually the first things to go, but eventually cherished heirlooms and other treasured possessions—anything not needed to live—had to be left to go to ruin.

Food on the Trail

Before setting out, most overlanders stocked up on staples such as flour, sugar, dried beans and fruit, cornmeal, and rice, as recommended in the guidebooks. They supplemented their provisions with game and other foods along the trail.

Buffalo provided the emigrants with plenty of fresh meat until the trains passed out of their range. The animals roved over the plains in herds of hundreds and thousands. Sometimes the plains were black with the great beasts as far as the eye could see. Many of the overlanders witnessed buffalo stampedes and never, as long as they lived, forgot the sight, the sound, and the awesome feeling it engendered. Because of the density of the buffalo herds, it was easy for even an inexpert shot to bring one down. Buffalo hunting was a great sport among the emigrants, and they engaged in it as much for the fun of it as for the food.

Antelope was another abundant food source, but it took a good marksman to hit one of these fleet animals. Jackrabbits, deer, mountain sheep, ducks, sage hens, and grouse were also hunted for food. Fish were abundant in many of the rivers and streams—one was described as being thick with trout—and salmon were plentiful in western Idaho along the Snake River.

In summer, the emigrants' diet was supplemented with greens and wild berries picked along the way. Many overlanders took along milk cows. As long as there was fresh milk, there

was also fresh butter; milk was put into a suitable container and churned by the constant jolting of the wagon. Saleratus (baking soda) could be found in quantity around the edges of some alkali ponds.

Cooking proved to be no problem for the emigrants, even without a stove, or wood for fuel. A fire pit—a narrow trench dug in the earth about a foot deep and two or three feet long—served remarkably well for the task. Unless the cook had a few metal rods to lay across the top of the trench to form a grate, the opening was made slightly smaller than the width of the smallest cooking utensil so it rested on the edges of the trench.

On the treeless prairie, an excellent source of fuel was provided by the millions of buffalo that roamed the area. Buffalo chips—dried dung—burned with very little odor and made a hot fire. At first, when the pioneer women had to gather the chips in their aprons, they thought it a disagreeable task, but it soon became accepted as a routine part of trail life.

Travel Aids

In the early years of the migration, the journey from Independence to the Willamette Valley took anywhere from five to six months. As the Oregon Trail became more heavily used, ferries and bridges sprang up at river crossings, and more trading posts and forts were built. These helped to shorten the travel time by as much as a month. No longer were the emigrants

held up at the rivers because of high water, repairs to wagons could be made quickly and conveniently, and most important, trail-worn draft animals could be traded for fresh ones, thus avoiding long layovers to rest the teams.

A toll was charged for the use of each bridge and ferry, and it was a lucrative business for the operator of the facility. Seeing how a quick profit could be made, some wily overlanders halted their own journey long enough to slap together some kind of a raft to serve as a ferry and collected their own fees. The ferriage ranged from one to eight dollars. Many emigrants thought this was exorbitant and, rather than pay, chose to ford the river. Some ferry operators took exception to this and tried to dissuade them at gunpoint. There are a few recorded incidents of pioneers or ferry operators being killed in these confrontations.

It was not only at the river crossings that the overlanders were rankled. They considered the prices for supplies at the trading posts too high. Most held a low opinion of the traders and believed, correctly in some cases, that they were excessively lining their own pockets. There were also mobile entrepreneurs with goods-laden wagons who traveled along with the emigrant trains, ready to supply them with whatever they needed, as long as they had cold cash to pay for it.

Indians

As potential emigrants contemplated the overland journey from their safe farms, villages, and towns, the possibility of meeting hostile Indians was one of their greatest concerns. They all expected to have some sort of confrontation with the "savages" and worried about coming through unscathed and unscalped.

Their fears were largely unfounded. The incidence of Indian attacks was greatly exaggerated. Of the nearly 300,000 pioneers who began the overland migration, fewer than 400 were killed by Indians. Most violent encounters were precipitated by the whites themselves.

Almost universally, whites believed they were superior to Indians. This attitude, coupled with a lack of knowledge about the Indians and their customs and habits, caused most of the trouble. In some cases, when an Indian was perceived to have committed a social slight, or engaged in playing a harmless prank, or misbehaved in some manner, intentional or not, that was enough cause for him to be shot.

Some emigrants started out with the aim to "get me an Injun" and wantonly murdered one or more at the first opportunity. This brought retaliation from the Indians, though it was not often against the wagon train of the perpetrator, but against the next train the Indians encountered. These seemingly random Indian attacks inflamed the whites and, in turn, caused more retaliatory killings.

Generally, the Indians along the trail were helpful and friendly. Many Indians provided services or supplies the pioneers needed—for a price, of course, usually trade goods. They also operated ferries, helped drive livestock across rivers, and rounded up cattle that had wandered away from campsites. Some Indian women made a thriving business of supplying moccasins to emigrants whose shoes had worn out; sooner or later this happened to all of them.

The overlanders engaged in trading with nearly all the tribes they encountered along the trail. A red shirt or other piece of clothing was often exchanged for fresh salmon along the Snake River. A trinket or food might be offered for some simple service performed. When an emigrant's horse was worn out, the Indians could be counted on to have horses to trade. Where horses were concerned, though, the whites nearly always got the worst of the deal.

Seeing the Elephant

Many of the emigrants started their journey with trepidation. In addition to the rumors about Indians, guidebooks and newspaper accounts written by those who had made the trip told of cholera and other diseases, dangerous river crossings, the dreaded pass through the Rocky Mountains, the cold and wet, hunger and thirst, and the frequent deaths on the trail.

When any of these things, singly or combined, happened to the pioneers and upset them to the point where they felt they could not bear it, it was said that they had "seen the elephant." If an emigrant saw too much of the mythical beast that supposedly ranged far and wide over the West, it was often cause for abandoning the whole venture and turning back. The elephant was not real, but the things it stood for were.

Death on the Trail

The number of emigrant deaths from disease and accident has been estimated to be about 15,000. Disease accounted for nine out of ten deaths. Often less than a week had gone by after leaving Independence before a burial was held. A wagon train that made it all the way to Oregon without losing one of its party was luckier than most.

Asiatic cholera, contracted from drinking infected water, claimed many lives. Its victims usually died within hours after the first symptoms appeared. There was no known treatment. If the victims survived, they were deathly ill for a few days.

Accidents also caused a great number of deaths. Many wagon trains were traveling arsenals. The emigrants had armed themselves to be prepared for Indian attacks and to shoot game. But most of them knew little or nothing about firearms and probably could not have hit their target in a critical situation. Many had a habit of grasping their guns by the barrel, mishandling that often resulted in serious wounds or death. One ill-starred fellow had managed to fire at and hit a wolf. In his excitement, after hastily reloading, he dropped his gun. It fell against a rock, discharged, and put a bullet through its owner's heart.

Wagon accidents were quite common. Many children were killed or maimed when they jumped down from the moving wagon and fell under the wheels. Drownings at river fords also took their toll. And humans and animals were killed during frequent cattle stampedes.

Cecilia Emily McMillen Adams faithfully recorded what she saw as she traveled to Oregon in 1852:

> *June 18, Passed 21 new made graves today.*
> *It makes it seem very gloomy to us to see*
> *so many of the emigrants buried on the*
> *plains.*
> *June 19, Passed 13 graves today.*
> *June 20, Passed 10 graves.*
> *June 22, Passed 7 graves. If we should go by*
> *all the camping grounds, we should see five*
> *times as many graves as we do now.*
> *June 23, Passed 21 graves.*

Although there were graves aplenty along the Oregon Trail, few were marked. In many instances, the departed were buried hurriedly, with scarcely any formalities, so the train would not be held up. Some of the graves were marked with a stake or wooden cross, when wood was available. Less commonly, a rock carved with the deceased's name marked the grave. In many instances, there was no time to fabricate even a simple marker. But when Susan Hail died, her devoted husband could not bear the thought of her resting in an unmarked grave and went back to St. Joseph to have a proper headstone carved. He transported it to the grave site—a distance of over two hundred miles—in a wheelbarrow.

It was erroneously believed that Indians would dig up graves to rob the deceased of their clothing. For this reason, as well as to prevent wolves from unearthing the remains, some of the dead were interred in the middle of the trail itself. Wagons were driven over the grave to tamp down the earth and leave no evidence that anyone had been buried there.

The End of the Trail

As the emigrants neared the end of the Oregon Trail, great numbers of them ran out of provisions and were near starvation. Others were exhausted or sick. Many were destitute, having lost their wagons and belongings and used up their savings paying tolls and ferry charges.

It was common for established Oregon residents to mount relief expeditions to aid those just arriving. Concerned and charitable settlers regularly took pack trains from The Dalles, a town on the Columbia River, to intercept companies of overlanders and help them along the final miles, doing what they could to ease their suffering.

Whether the emigrants traversed the Oregon Trail with few or an abundance of problems, for most of them the overland journey was the most significant experience of their lives. It also affected the thousands yet to come—these pioneers opened the way that made the settlement of the West possible. Those hardy souls who established the Oregon Trail helped shape and unify the country. Largely because of them, the contiguous United States reaches from the Atlantic Ocean to the Pacific Ocean.

CHAPTER ONE

Missouri and Kansas

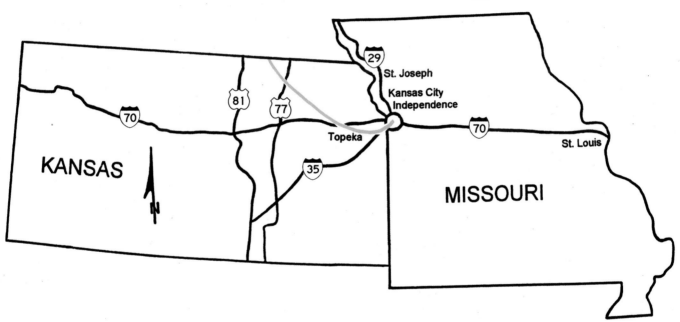

Two main branches of the Oregon Trail led from Independence, Missouri, the southern-most branch following the established Santa Fe Trail.

On each branch, just a few miles from the departure point, the untried oxen, their inexperienced drivers, the excited children, and the apprehensive adults crossed their first river, the Blue, and made the pull up the sloping embankment on the other side. It was the beginning of their seasoning for the long road that lay ahead.

Crossed the Blue soon in the morning.

—Virgil Pringle, May 8, 1846

SANTA FE TRAIL–OREGON TRAIL, WILLIAM E. MINOR PARK, KANSAS CITY, MISSOURI*

I made a very thorough examination of the Blue Mound and, if it had not been such an immense mass, should have left it believing that it was the work of man.

—John Minto, June 1844

Appearing strangely out of place, Blue Mound rose out of the flat land around it like a giant swelling. Although it was only a few days from Independence, coming upon it was an occasion for the pioneers because it was the first distinct height of land they saw.

BLUE MOUND, SOUTH OF LAWRENCE, KANSAS

*The Vermillion is the worst stream
we have crossed, the banks are so
steep and muddy and rocky.*

—Rebecca Ketcham, 1853

An epidemic of Asiatic cholera killed at least fifty emigrants who were camped near the Red Vermillion River Crossing. This lofty elm, perhaps a descendant of another tree that grew here over 150 years ago, was a magnificent memorial for the victims buried here, most in unmarked graves. (The tree has been destroyed by a succession of recent storms, and now only a giant stump remains.)

EMIGRANT GRAVESTONE AT THE RED VERMILLION RIVER CROSSING

ELM TREE AT THE RED VERMILLION RIVER CROSSING, EAST OF LOUISVILLE, KANSAS

After Edwin Bryant named the place Alcove Spring, George M. McKinstry carved the name in eight-inch-high letters on a large flat stone above the spring's runoff. Others incised their names into the limestone.

The spring hollow was heavily and variously timbered with oak, cottonwood, walnut, and sycamore trees. When most of the wagon trains arrived, the trees were greening with the delicate colors of spring, the grass was lush and plentiful, and wildflowers blossomed everywhere. Lovely as it was, this site, only a few days' journey from Independence, carried its burden of sorrow. On the heights around it, safe from any flooding, are the graves of many who succumbed to cholera.

In 1846, when the family of Sarah Keyes set off westward, the plucky seventy-year-old woman steadfastly refused to be left behind in Illinois. Although her health was failing, she was determined to travel with her daughter as far as she could. Her final resting place is beneath a large oak on a hillock above Alcove Spring.

ROCK CARVED BY GEORGE M. MCKINSTRY

. . . a most beautiful spring and a fall of water of 12 feet.

—George M. McKinstry, May 30, 1846

ALCOVE SPRING, BLUE RAPIDS, KANSAS

The Hollenberg Ranch House was built on the Oregon Trail in 1857, near the junction with the trail from St. Joseph, Missouri. It was used as a trading post and later served as a Pony Express station. Houses and other structures, though few in number, were not an uncommon sight in the beginning miles of the Oregon Trail. But farther on, when such an ordinary thing as a house was seen again, it was invariably mentioned in the pioneers' journals.

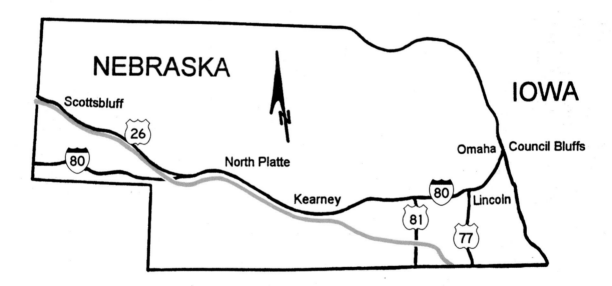

Imagine the ocean, when the waves are rolling mountains high, becoming solid and covered with beautiful green grass and you have some faint idea of it.

—Rebecca Ketcham, May 1853

By the time the emigrants reached Rock Creek, they were truly on the prairie. From the low brows of the gently sloping hills, they could see for miles in all directions. This landscape evoked many references to the sea in the emigrants' writings.

WAGON REPRODUCTION, ROCK CREEK STATION STATE HISTORICAL PARK,
EAST OF FAIRBURY, NEBRASKA

The Platte River, east of where its northern and southern branches fork, was unlike any river the overlanders had ever seen. It was randomly wide and narrow, shallow and deep, but mostly shallow, with stagnant pools, mudflats, and sandbars, and always, unvaryingly, muddy.

The Platte was the subject of much ridicule: "Too thick to drink and too thin to plow." "A mile wide and a foot deep." "The river that flows upside down."

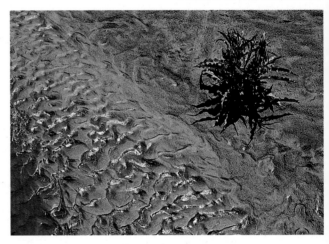

PLATTE RIVER MUDFLATS

Perhaps this is one of the most remarkable rivers in the world. Like the Nile it runs hundreds of miles through a sandy desert. The valley of this stream is from fifteen to twenty miles wide, a smooth level plain, and the river generally runs in the middle of it, from west to east. The course of this stream is more uniform than any I have ever seen. It scarcely ever makes a bend. This river has low, sand banks, with sandy bottom, and the water is muddy.

—Peter H. Burnett, 1853

PLATTE RIVER, KEARNEY STATE RECREATION AREA, SOUTHEAST OF KEARNEY, NEBRASKA

FORT KEARNY STATE HISTORICAL PARK,
SOUTHEAST OF KEARNEY, NEBRASKA

Fort Kearny was the first fort built solely for the protection of the ever-swelling tide of westward-bound pioneers. (The spelling of the city and county is now Kearney, but the park retains the original spelling, Kearny.) The unfortified outpost was completed in 1848; the cottonwood trees planted on the parade ground that same year still stand today.

At present it consists of a number of long, low buildings constructed principally of adobe, or sun dried bricks, with nearly flat roofs of brush.

—A. J. McCall, May 29, 1849

BLACKSMITH SHOP, FORT KEARNY STATE HISTORICAL PARK, SOUTHEAST OF KEARNEY, NEBRASKA

The Oregon Trail closely followed the south side of the Platte River. At O'Fallon's Bluff, the river elbowed its way around the base of the hill, leaving no room for wagons. They had to be taken up and over the bluff, and there the wheels cut deep swales.

On one occasion today we had to retreat over the bluff on account of the river.

—Henry Allyn, June 9, 1853

O'Fallon's Bluff, Interstate 80 rest area between Hershey and Sutherland, Nebraska*

Sooner or later the Platte, now called the South Platte, had to be crossed. Because of the river's width, which varied from three-quarters of a mile to a mile and a half, and its ever-changing channels, it could not be bridged. And because of its depth, only inches in places, ferries could not be used.

Crossings were made wherever conditions and whim dictated, but the majority of wagon trains forded the river in the vicinity of the Lower California Crossing. The place got its name during the gold rush years; the Upper California Crossing was about twenty miles west.

Many emigrants feared crossing the Platte because they had heard that the channel bed was entirely quicksand. If any quicksand existed, it was not channel-wide and caused no serious problems. Nothing and no one was ever swallowed up by quicksand.

We made a good forenoon drive and moved in sight of the lower crossing of the south fork of the Platte. We succeeded in crossing it. We blocked up some 10 inches, doubled teams, drove and waded, and in about three hours we got over.

—John B. Spencer, June 16, 1852

Lower California Crossing, South Platte River, West of Brule, Nebraska

Had a pretty hard pull up the bluff and then found a gently rolling prairie.

—James Field, June 8, 1845

After crossing the south fork of the Platte River, the wagons carved many swales in the earth as the teams strained up the incline of the nearly two-mile-long California Hill.

CALIFORNIA HILL, WEST OF BRULE, NEBRASKA*

Trail route atop Windlass Hill, near Ash Hollow State
Historical Park, south of Lewellen, Nebraska*

WINDLASS HILL, ASH HOLLOW STATE HISTORICAL PARK,
SOUTH OF LEWELLEN, NEBRASKA*

Here we found our first hill to go down that was worthy to be called a hill.

—Andrew Jackson Wigle, 1853

There had been a few sloping river and stream banks to slow the overlanders' progress, but here at Windlass Hill was the first long, steep descent of the Oregon Trail. The inviting, tree-shaded Ash Hollow could be seen just ahead at the bottom of the hill. One emigrant remarked that it seemed impossible for such heavily laden wagons to descend safely, but most reached the bottom without mishap.

No record exists of any windlasses being used here, and the origin of the name is a mystery. To slow the descent of the wagons, all available men and women held back on ropes tied to each wagon.

39

This is a beautiful place with high bluffs on all sides, there are some ash trees from which it takes its name. The greatest profusion of wild roses is in full bloom and many other flowers; the sides of the bluffs were literally covered and the air heavy with the odor of them. I was enchanted and could scarcely tear myself away.

—Esther Belle Hanna, June 5, 1852

Set among harsh limestone bluffs were cool springs in a sylvan glade known as Ash Hollow. This was an oasis where the pioneers lingered after their adventurous plunge down Windlass Hill.

WILD ROSES IN ASH HOLLOW
STATE HISTORICAL PARK

40

ASH HOLLOW STATE HISTORICAL PARK, SOUTH OF LEWELLEN, NEBRASKA

The Oregon Trail followed the south side of the Platte River for about 150 miles. After the trail crossed the unbroken plain between the Lower California Crossing and Ash Hollow, it struck the north fork of the Platte. It followed this branch for another 250 miles before crossing the river for the last time, just before the river made a great bend to the south, where it flowed from its distant source in the Rocky Mountains.

Unlike the lethargic, shallow South Platte, the North Platte ran full, fast, deep, and cold.

The winding Platte, the scene adorned by a setting sun, was sublime beyond description of a feeble pen.

—Andrew S. McClure, June 5, 1853

North Platte River, southeast of Lewellen, Nebraska

Courthouse and Jail Rocks, so named because of their supposed resemblance to the architectural style of certain municipal buildings, were the first of the great formations that the emigrants saw along the Oregon Trail. The rocks rose majestically from the level, otherwise featureless prairie.

Many of the overlanders came from forested states east of the Missouri and Mississippi Rivers, so being able to see for miles was a new experience, and it altered their ability to judge distance. While these formations appeared to be just a short distance away, they were actually several miles from the trail. Many who attempted to reach the landmarks turned back after several hours because the rocks still looked no closer than they had when they started out.

At a distance of 15 miles it presents a very fine appearance—seeming like a great regular structure of brick with a low dome.

—S. H. Taylor, June 1853

COURTHOUSE AND JAIL ROCKS, SOUTH OF BRIDGEPORT, NEBRASKA

When approaching it, it takes a variety of forms—sometimes that of an old ruin, then a very sharp cone; but, after all, more the shape of a chimney than anything else.

—A. J. McCall, June 13, 1849

Most of the emigrants caught sight of Chimney Rock when it was still two days' travel ahead of them. It was easy to see the stark, solitary formation that reached over three hundred feet into the clear, clean air of the prairie.

CHIMNEY ROCK, SOUTH OF BAYARD, NEBRASKA

During the first years of the migration west, the easiest way through the towering rocks that stretched for miles across what is now western Nebraska was through a sweeping valley leading to Robidoux Pass.

One of the Robidoux clan, fur traders from St. Joseph, Missouri, operated a trading post and blacksmith shop in the valley until a better route was found through Mitchell Pass, a short distance to the north.

Good springs and grass near the trading post of a fur company.

—John G. Glenn, June 27, 1852

Robidoux Pass, west of Gering, Nebraska*

Scotts Bluff was named for fur trapper Hiram Scott. The story of the unfortunate Scott intrigued the pioneers, and many wrote about it in great detail in their diaries. In 1828 Scott and two companions were traveling by boat down the North Platte River toward the bluff, where the three were to rendezvous with other trappers. When they were some sixty miles west of their destination, Scott became ill. His unfeeling comrades, sure his death was imminent, abandoned him. Scott made his torturous way alone to the rendezvous location to find only the long-dead ashes of the trappers' campfires. There was no help for him now. He crawled to a spring at the base of the bluff, where he died. His bones were found months later, picked clean by wolves.

They are beetling cliffs of indurated clay, bearing resemblance to towers, castles, and fortified cities.

—A. J. McCall, June 14, 1849

Eagle Rock, Scotts Bluff National Monument, Gering, Nebraska

MITCHELL PASS, SCOTTS BLUFF NATIONAL MONUMENT, GERING, NEBRASKA*

The broad break in the massive sandstone and siltstone ridge of Scotts Bluff is Mitchell Pass. After cresting the gentle rise of the pass, the emigrants often had their first view of what many of them thought were the Rocky Mountains. What loomed on the far horizon, however, were the Laramie Mountains. The range, including Laramie Peak, over ten thousand feet high, was visible from the pass, though it was more than a hundred miles away.

This morning the road passed over the ridge from which we saw some of the peaks of the mountains.

—David E. Pease, June 2, 1849

52

CHAPTER THREE
Wyoming

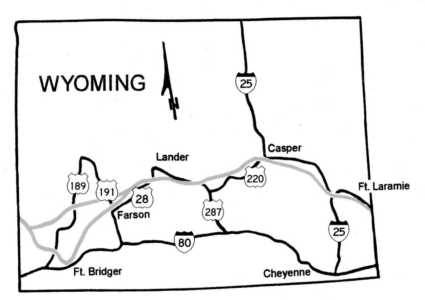

"Old Bedlam," built as officers' quarters in 1849, Fort Laramie
National Historic Site, west of Fort Laramie, Wyoming

Fort Laramie was a popular place with Indians, fur trappers, and overlanders. A sizable Indian encampment of tipis, often numbering in the hundreds, was always in evidence around the fort. These colorful dwellings were a counterpoint to the many plain frame and adobe buildings that served the fort.

Here, the pioneers could purchase supplies of all kinds and make repairs at the blacksmith shop. Here, too, was one of the few dependable post offices along the route.

There is one two-story house very well finished at Laramie, and one large frame just raised, and several clay buildings whitewashed on the outside, which give it quite the appearance of a village in a savage land.

—Orange Gaylord, June 4, 1853

FORT LARAMIE NATIONAL HISTORIC SITE, WEST OF FORT LARAMIE, WYOMING

REGISTER CLIFF, SOUTH OF GUERNSEY, WYOMING*

The overlanders inscribed their names in many places along the trail, but it was not ego that motivated them to do so. Register Cliff, like many other places father west, served as a message board for family and friends in following trains. An emigrant's name and the date he or she was there confirmed to those behind that the person had been alive on that date. It also let them know approximately how many days apart they were.

Alva H. Unthank, in good health, neatly scratched his name in the soft sandstone. Within days he was buried, a few miles away—another victim of the quick-striking cholera.

We came along the base of a large bluff that was covered up as far as a person could reach with names and dates of those that have passed this way.

—Delila Berintha Saunders, July 9, 1866

EMIGRANTS' NAMES CARVED IN REGISTER CLIFF,
SOUTH OF GUERNSEY, WYOMING

The low, rough ridges west of Fort Laramie presented the most rugged terrain yet encountered by the emigrants. They were named the Black Hills because of the dark green juniper trees growing on them, which appeared black from a distance. Deep Rut Hill is on the western perimeter of the Black Hills.

The exposed rock atop this sandstone ridge attests to the volume of travel over the Oregon Trail more than in any other location. Year after year, as wagons by the thousands rolled over the rise, they carved their own monument to the western migration. A human hand could not have done it so well or so eloquently.

The top of the ridge is scarred with many ruts, but the main track was worn to a depth of five feet. Few emigrants remarked on what came to be called Deep Rut Hill. During the early years of travel on the trail, the ruts were not worn deeply into the rock, but it is a wonder that some of the later travelers did not write about the shoulder-deep sides of the trail.

The road through these hills is, of necessity, very circuitous; winding about as it must to avoid the steeps, ravines and rocks.

—Overton Johnson and William H. Winter, 1843

DEEP RUT HILL, SOUTH OF GUERNSEY, WYOMING*

We are now in sight of the highest portion of earth that ever I looked upon.

—William Cornell, June 24, 1852

Laramie Peak had loomed ahead for days, but the Oregon Trail did not cross the Laramie Mountains. It followed the northern curve of the range, on flat land. The closest the emigrants came to Laramie Peak was thirty miles.

Laramie Peak, from south of Wendover, Wyoming*

With the Black Hills behind them, the emigrants spent a few days crossing an area laced with pleasant, easily forded streams providing plentiful drinking water. There was usually good grass and even some wood for campfires.

We encamped on a most beautiful stream, called the La Bonte.

—A. J. McCall, June 20, 1849

LA BONTE CROSSING, SOUTH OF DOUGLAS, WYOMING*

Just west of La Bonte Crossing, the color of the earth and some of the rock formations changed from grey-brown to brick red—this was new and exotic to the pioneers.

The rocks being of a reddish cast present a beautiful appearance a short distance off.

—Orange Gaylord, June 7, 1853

RED EARTH COUNTRY, SOUTH OF DOUGLAS, WYOMING

Up near the high bluff there is an arch of solid stone over this river, 40 or 50 feet wide and 15 feet high. I passed up the river, rode through beneath the arch, and viewed with delight the grand works of nature.

—J. R. Starr, June 26, 1850

The graceful arch over La Prele Creek was two miles off the main route of the Oregon Trail. The emigrants were interested in seeing all the natural curiosities, and walking all day never seemed to dampen their enthusiasm for exploring further once they arrived at the day's campsite. If there was something to be seen, they wanted to have a look at it.

AYRES NATURAL BRIDGE STATE PARK, WEST OF DOUGLAS, WYOMING

After the emigrants crossed the North Platte River, just east of Rock Avenue, the sagebrush-covered country began in earnest. The "avenue" was a smooth, level area just wide enough for wagons to pass through in single file. On either side lay jagged, lichen-decorated sandstone slabs scattered helter-skelter.

It is about one hundred and fifty yards long and is composed of stone piled up on either side of the road some distance above the surface of the road, forming a kind of pass or defile.

—Andrew S. McClure, June 27, 1853

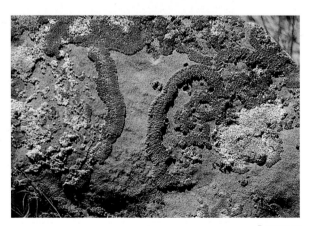

LICHEN

ROCK AVENUE, SOUTHWEST OF BESSEMER BEND, WYOMING

The trail through this land was hard on livestock. There was little forage and even less drinkable water. Ponds, pools, and springs were frequent on this part of the route, but thirsty beasts had to be kept away from them, as they were highly alkaline. Drinking this water meant almost certain death, as testified by the whitening bones of cattle around the ponds.

These are very poisonous and a great many cattle died from its effects. We did not let our cattle taste it, fearing its consequences. Passing on from here we saw a great many cattle lying dead and a great many that had been left which were yet alive.

—J. R. Starr, July 1, 1850

ALKALI PONDS, SOUTHWEST OF ROCK AVENUE

We found a beautiful spring, of very cold clear water, rising in a little green valley, through which its water flowed about one mile.

—Overton Johnson and William H. Winter, July 25, 1843

At last, among the waste of sagebrush and alkali, the overlanders reached Willow Spring, where the cattle could be allowed to drink to their hearts' content. The spring provided a never-ending supply of cool, pure water, and around it was abundant sweet grass.

WILLOW SPRING, SOUTHWEST OF ROCK AVENUE

When, on the Fourth of July in 1830, an American Fur Company expedition found themselves at this rounded, granite, behemoth of a rock, they decided to name it in honor of the occasion, Independence Day. Because many emigrants carved their names on Independence Rock, they called it "The Great Register of the Desert."

The area around the rock was a favorite campground on the trail. The gentle, meandering Sweetwater River, with an abundance of grass growing alongside it, flowed around the south side of the rock.

There is at least a million names of emigrants on the rock, some are in small type and some very large.

—William Kahler, July 6, 1852

EMIGRANT'S NAME CARVED ON INDEPENDENCE ROCK

INDEPENDENCE ROCK STATE HISTORIC SITE, WEST OF ALCOVA, WYOMING

Within sight of Independence Rock was another source of wonderment to the emigrants—Devils Gate. The Sweetwater River runs through the shadowed declivity. Ever the tourists, many of the pioneers felt compelled to scramble to the top of the rocks for the view. Some even inched their way to the very edge of the rift and peered straight down onto the river, nearly four hundred feet below.

Everybody must take a look at it. Here the waters of the Sweetwater rush and foam through a narrow passage two hundred feet below and it takes strong nerves to look down into the rushing waters.

—George Miller West, 1852

DEVILS GATE, NEAR INDEPENDENCE ROCK

*Cut Rock . . . grass in abundance,
sagebrush and willows for fuel.*

—O. Allen, 1858

Split Rock, or Cut Rock, as some of the emigrants called it, was yet another interesting formation along the Sweetwater River. It rose a thousand feet above the trail and came into view just after passing Devils Gate.

SPLIT ROCK, WEST OF DEVILS GATE

Three different wagon routes led through this area, two of them in deep sand. The third, considered to be the least difficult, followed the Sweetwater River. The river filled a defile, so that scarcely anything that could be called a bank existed on either side. This necessitated zigzagging the wagons through the passage and entailed three crossings of the river.

Today we have crossed the Sweetwater River three times, there being scarce a mile-and-a-half between the first and last crossing. The rocks came so near the river, first on one side, then on the other, we were obliged to cross to get along.

—Rebecca Ketcham, July 1853

THREE CROSSINGS OF THE SWEETWATER, NORTHEAST OF JEFFREY CITY, WYOMING

We dug in the earth about 12 inches, and found chinks of ice. We carried it along till about noon, and made some lemonade for dinner. It relished first rate.

—George Belshaw, July 4, 1853

Ice Slough, a shallow basin at an altitude of six thousand feet, held an assortment of ponds and springs. Some sections were covered with a thick, insulating layer of turf that preserved the winter ice. Some emigrants dug up the ice— a most welcome refreshment during the hottest months of the year.

ICE SLOUGH, WEST OF JEFFREY CITY, WYOMING

Rocky Ridge was a very rough section of the trail. Rocks of all sizes, from pebbles to boulders, covered the landscape, making it impossible to pick a way around them. They had to roll the wagons over them, and eventually the hundreds of wheels carved an eternal record of their passing.

~ ... ascended the high hill
... and ascended another very stony and rough,
requiring the care of the teamsters.

—J. Goldsborough Bruff, July 31, 1849

WAGON RUT CARVED IN ROCK, ROCKY RIDGE, WEST OF ICE SLOUGH*

ROCKY RIDGE, WEST OF ICE SLOUGH*

After months of climbing steadily and imperceptibly, the emigrants reached, at seven thousand feet, South Pass, the crossing of the Continental Divide and the halfway point on their two-thousand-mile journey.

The overlanders had heard of this pass, but most of them imagined it to be a narrow defile. How could it be otherwise in the heart of the Rockies? They were amazed when they beheld the nearly flat plain, stretching for miles in all directions, that was the top of the continent. It looked no different from the hundreds of miles of sagebrush-covered desert they had already passed through. A glance northward, however, to the myriad, white-capped, lofty peaks of the Wind River Range, looming large even though some twenty miles away, erased any doubt the pioneers may have had about their whereabouts.

This was further confirmed by the weather here, where the earth appeared to meet the sky. It was the rare company of overlanders who did not experience violent storms pelting them with rain, hail, sleet, or snow, or endure bitter night cold at the Pacific Springs campground, just west of the pass.

We began to ascend a very gradual elevation until we reach[ed] a broad and naked plain with high, rugged, cold, blue mountain peaks to the right. The ascent is so gradual that it was difficult to fix the culminating point.

—A. J. McCall, July 5, 1849

OPPOSITE: SOUTH PASS, SOUTHWEST OF SOUTH PASS CITY, WYOMING*

The colorful formation of Plume Rocks, which are not rocks at all but a conglomerate of clay and pebbles, stands alone in the landscape. It is the only formation of its kind for miles around. Although shaped by the elements, it looks as if it might have been sculpted by an artist, who placed it here to be set off against the backdrop of the Wind River Mountains.

. . . on our right, about 300 yards distant, some low clay bluffs, of a dark dingy red hue, and singularly plume-formed projections on top.

—J. Goldsborough Bruff, August 3, 1849

PLUME ROCKS, EAST OF FARSON, WYOMING

Our company separated today, eight wagons taking the common route and the others . . . took what is called the cutoff.

—James Mather, July 16, 1846

Shortly after passing Plume Rocks, the emigrants reached the Parting of the Ways. There they had the choice of continuing on the main trail to the southwest or taking the Sublette Cutoff.

THE PARTING OF THE WAYS, MAIN OREGON TRAIL TO THE LEFT,
SUBLETTE CUTOFF TO THE RIGHT.*

We take what is known as Sublette's Cutoff, and at Big Sandy camp and rest, making preparations to cross the desert . . . a dry sandy plain without grass or water. We break camp at two A.M. and commence this dry journey.

—George Miller West, June 1852

The Sublette Cutoff was a shortcut from the main trail that saved a hundred miles, but for those who took it, it meant a fifty-mile trek across the most desolate and hostile land they had encountered thus far. About ten miles west of the Parting of the Ways on the cutoff route, the travelers came to the Big Sandy River. Here they stored water in every available container and gathered as much grass as possible to feed the animals, for ahead of them lay a barren land, devoid of water, grass, and shade. From the river, the emigrants saw the slender ribbon of trail reaching westward through a seemingly endless plain of sagebrush.

It was more than many of the emigrants could tolerate to traverse these desert miles in the intense heat of the day, so some trains made the crossing at night. Even so, animals died by the score. Many of the pioneers expected to "see the elephant" on this stretch, and many did.

SUBLETTE FLAT ON THE SUBLETTE CUTOFF, NORTH OF FARSON, WYOMING*

By the time the emigrants reached the Green River, after the arduous desert crossing, they were weary beyond imagining. Yet to reach the river's abundance of water and grass, they had to summon the energy to take the wagons down a steep cliff. Before the first ferry was established in 1847, the pioneers had to ford the river on their own to continue on.

We found our way into the river bottom by a precipitous and difficult descent from the top of a very high bluff.

—James P. Pritchard, June 21, 1849

GREEN RIVER CROSSING ON THE SUBLETTE CUTOFF, SOUTH OF LA BARGE, WYOMING

EMIGRANT SPRING ON THE SUBLETTE CUTOFF,
NORTHEAST OF KEMMERER, WYOMING

Once across the Green River, the emigrants left the flat desert and set off on a fairly easy trail through low mountains. After the river crossing, it wasn't far to Emigrant Spring, a campsite with water, grass, and timber. From there, the pioneers had only about a two-day journey before they rejoined the main Oregon Trail.

Those who opted to stay on the main trail instead of taking the Sublette Cutoff found an unchanging, desolate landscape stretching ahead for mile after dreary mile. Perhaps some wondered whether they had made the right choice. To avoid traveling in a cloud of dust, the emigrants lined up the wagons abreast instead of in single file. The column they formed was sometimes over a mile wide.

My companions pronounce this as the most God forsaken country they ever saw. Destitute of timber, of grass, of game—even water scarce. They cannot see for what purpose it was raised from the sea.

—A. J. McCall, July 9, 1849

LITTLE COLORADO DESERT, SOUTHWEST OF FARSON, WYOMING*

The Green River roiled and rumbled its way southward from its birthplace in the high, snowy Wind River Mountains to the north. Crossing it was a difficult and dangerous undertaking. In the early years of the trail, before a ferry was established, the river had to be forded—there was no other choice. The only safe crossing was on a submerged, narrow gravel bar. Missing the bar could mean disaster for people, wagons, and livestock.

. . . a cold swift mountain stream, 18 rods wide. Tumbles and rolls through the mountain like a milltail.

—George Belshaw, July 19, 1853

LOMBARD FERRY ON THE GREEN RIVER, NORTH OF GREEN RIVER, WYOMING

~ . . . the shape of a large temple and decorated with all kinds of images: gods, and goddesses, everything that has been the subject of the sculptor: all kinds of animals and creeping things.

—John Boardman, August 12, 1843

Standing alone on the desert was the singular formation known as Church Buttes. The wind and the weather had carved its green and gray sandstone into fantastic and grotesque shapes.

CHURCH BUTTES, SOUTHWEST OF GRANGER, WYOMING

RECONSTRUCTION OF FORT BRIDGER, FORT BRIDGER
STATE HISTORIC SITE, FORT BRIDGER, WYOMING

In early trail days, Fort Bridger was not a military fort but a palisaded trading post and blacksmith shop owned by Jim Bridger and Louis Vasquez. From the Parting of the Ways, the main Oregon Trail veered southwest to a point on the Blacks Fork of the Green River, then angled off to the northwest until reaching the Bear River Divide. Fort Bridger was at the point of this vee.

We found Fort Bridger a small stockade used as a rendezvous for trappers and Indian trade.

—J. M. Harrison, 1846

Fort Bridger was built in a lovely, well-watered valley with the snow-covered peaks of the Uinta Mountains to the south. It was opportunely situated to capitalize on trade with the overlanders and their ongoing need for blacksmith services.

This is a pretty place to see in such a barren country. Perhaps there is a thousand acres of level land covered with grass interspersed with beautiful strong brooks and plenty of timber.
—Elizabeth Dixon Smith, August 9, 1850

STREAM, FORT BRIDGER STATE HISTORIC SITE, FORT BRIDGER, WYOMING

MUDDY CREEK, SOUTH OF KEMMERER, WYOMING

Once the emigrants crossed Muddy Creek—a difficult ford when running with snowmelt—they had a short respite from sagebrush flats and desert heat in the Bear Mountains. The trail here was rugged and steep, but not difficult enough to keep the travelers from enjoying the change of scenery.

Muddy Fork, a beautiful, clear stream, with plenty of good grass on its banks.

—Samuel Handsacker, July 14, 1853

104

CHAPTER FOUR

Idaho

The emigrants, most them farmers, beheld the Bear River Valley and thought it a paradise. If it had not been so far from other settlements, some would have made it the end of the trail and established themselves there to farm its fertile soil, joining the friendly, ebullient Shoshone Indians who lived happily along the river.

As the overlanders descended the heights of the Bear Mountains, the basin spread out before them—an emerald green jewel in a blue mountain setting. Lush grass grew everywhere, nurtured by the Bear River wandering extravagantly through the valley. The trail-weary pioneers tarried here to rest, to make repairs to wagons, to catch up on household tasks, and to partake of the bounty of the place. It provided wild berries and abundant game.

Thomas Fork, Bear River Valley, west of Border, Wyoming

Here we found pure water, sufficient for all of us and our cattle. Here we also found oceans of grass and thousands of acres of rich, level land covered with wild flax.

—P. V. Crawford, July 8, 1851

FLAX IN FLOWER

BEAR RIVER VALLEY, SOUTH OF MONTPELIER, IDAHO

Soda Springs was undoubtedly the greatest curiosity on the entire Oregon Trail. The emigrants were still traveling through the hospitable Bear River Valley, with nothing to concern them for at least a few miles more, so at the springs they could relax, marvel at its wonders, and sample its many-flavored waters. One traveler, a minister who evidently looked askance at the frolicking of his companions, said as he surveyed the scene, "Hell is not more than a mile from this place."

Mineral deposits shaped the otherworldly landscape of cones and craters, and among them lay hot springs, warm springs, and cold springs. Some tasted like soda water, others had a metallic flavor, and one had a taste likened to beer. The most captivating was Steamboat Spring, which sounded like a steamboat whistle as it gurgled, chuffed, and then exploded from its cone in a steaming geyser three feet high.

The water oozed from between the rocks, the surface of which was red as blood.

—Lucia Loraine Williams, July 5, 1851

SPRINGS, SODA SPRINGS, IDAHO

. . . within these basaltic walls, the clear cold waters of the river rush and roar.

—J. Goldsborough Bruff, August 18, 1849

At this landmark known as Sheep Rock, some of the pioneers bound for California headed southwest on the Hudspeth Cutoff.

SHEEP ROCK AT SODA POINT, SOUTHWEST OF SODA SPRINGS, IDAHO

West of Soda Springs the landscape changed dramatically; here began ancient lava fields. All the rock on the remainder of the trail—whether it was underlying vegetation, exposed in ragged black outcroppings and deeply cleft, sheer-sided rifts, or rising in towering mountain peaks— was of volcanic origin.

VOLCANIC LANDS WEST OF SODA SPRINGS, IDAHO

ALEXANDER CRATER, WEST OF SODA SPRINGS, IDAHO

This valley appears to have been sunk several feet and is full of chasms, from two to twenty feet wide, and of unknown depth. Volcanic rock is scattered over it, in large masses; and in many places it appears to have been upheaved from beneath. We passed on the left, a large, hollow mound, the crater of an extinguished volcano.

—Overton Johnson and William H. Winter, September 1843

From five miles away, the overlanders could see the white adobe walls of Fort Hall, situated on a level plain near the Snake River. Fort Hall was an outpost of the Hudson's Bay Company. Supplies brought from Astoria, on the Oregon coast, could be purchased here at what most emigrants thought were exorbitant prices.

Eighteen miles today took us to Fort Hall which stands upon the level bottom of Snake River with a fine pasturage and some timber around it. It is a good-sized fort, built like Fort Laramie of unburnt brick.

—James Field, July 1845

Reconstruction of Fort Hall, Pocatello, Idaho

Black, jagged, upthrusting rocks punctuated this landscape, where the Oregon Trail passed narrowly between the rough lava outcroppings. About a day's travel ahead was the Raft River, where the main trail to California branched off to the southwest.

Wagon trains traveled through this region for nearly twenty years without any interference from the Shoshone Indians. But in 1862, Indians waited among the concealing rocks close by the trail and set upon the unsuspecting emigrants of two different wagon trains. The Indians killed ten pioneers, wounded as many, looted the wagons, and ran off the livestock. After these attacks, the violence subsided.

Then we marched on about eight miles and came to a rock gap that the road passed through just wide enough for wagons.

—Absalom B. Harden, July 28, 1847

Massacre Rocks State Park, west of American Falls, Idaho

The river is generally difficult of access being shut in on either side with high bluffs of basaltic rock.

—J. M. Harrison, 1846

Reaching the water of the Snake River was often impossible because of its precipitous, sometimes vertical cliffs.

CAULDRON LINN, SNAKE RIVER, EAST OF MURTAUGH, IDAHO

Almost as if to make up for the austerity and sameness of its valley, the Snake River was graced with myriad waterfalls. The emigrants saw the falls that were near the trail, but they only heard the thunderous roar of more distant ones.

... produces a rumbling that may be heard several miles during the stillness of the night. The noise of the falls sounds like music in the ears of the lover of adventure.

—Andrew S. McClure, July 27, 1853

SHOSHONE FALLS, EAST OF TWIN FALLS, IDAHO

Poor camp and you have to drive cattle down a bluff to get water; you have to bring your using-water over a half-mile up the bluffs.

—Absalom B. Harden, July 1847

To cross Rock Creek, which flowed at the bottom of a chasm, the emigrants had to travel eight miles to the southwest, away from the Snake, to the only ford where the canyon walls were low enough to take wagons down.

ROCK CREEK, SOUTHEAST OF TWIN FALLS, IDAHO

Fine scenery on the opposite side of the river, rocks six or eight hundred feet high, fourteen distinct waterfalls pouring out from them, only two coming over the top.

—Rebecca Ketcham, August 1853

Another wonder of the trail was Thousand Springs, where cascades of quicksilver water burst forth from the face of basalt cliffs.

THOUSAND SPRINGS, SOUTH OF HAGERMAN, IDAHO

In coming down to the river bottom, there is a very steep hill.

—Joel Palmer, August 23, 1845

At last the Snake River escaped from the deep fissure of unassailable volcanic rock that had sliced through the land for nearly two hundred miles. Above Three Island Crossing the emigrants encountered a sagebrush-covered hill, which, though steep, the teams could negotiate without too much difficulty.

ABOVE THREE ISLAND CROSSING OF THE SNAKE RIVER,
NEAR GLENNS FERRY, IDAHO*

Because the Snake River ran between solid rock walls for most of its length, it picked up little sediment. It was the clearest river most of the emigrants had ever seen.

The Snake was generally six to eight feet deep at Three Island Crossing, but, because of its clarity, it appeared to be quite shallow. The deceptiveness of the water's depth, coupled with the swift current, made this one of the more treacherous river crossings on the trail. Guidebooks gave detailed instructions on how to avoid mishaps; nevertheless, men and animals drowned frequently here, and loaded wagons often capsized.

First we drive over a part of the river 100 yards wide to an island, then over another branch 75 yards wide to a second island; then we tied a string of wagons together by a chain. . . . We carried as many as 15 wagons at one time. The water was 10 inches up the wagons' beds in the deeper places. It was about 9000 yards across.

—William T. Newby, September 11, 1843

THREE ISLAND CROSSING STATE PARK, SOUTHWEST OF GLENNS FERRY, IDAHO

Those who did not ford the Snake River at Three Island Crossing continued along the south bank of the river. They encountered a bleak, parched land that made the so-called Great American Desert they had already traversed pale in comparison. Here were hub-deep sand, tremendous dunes, searing heat, and sparse, dry vegetation. Fortunately, the overlanders did not have to cross the dunes. They saw them rising a short distance to the south of the trail.

The most desolate country in the whole world. The region of the shadow of death.

—Samuel James, July 24, 1850

DESERT PLANT, BRUNEAU DUNES STATE PARK

Bruneau Dunes State Park, west of Hammett, Idaho

The emigrants who crossed the Snake at Three Island Crossing also had many miles of desert to traverse. Cattle died by the thousands in the wasteland. Already weak, they were done in by this stretch of trail without adequate food and water. Some emigrants described how the wagons rolled between banks of rotting, stinking carcasses. One woman wrote of holding a handkerchief to her nose, but it did not keep out the stench. Another complained that the campground was intolerable because of the many dead animals lying nearby.

A few miles ahead, in the valley of the Boise River, were grass and water. The cattle that survived the desert could refresh themselves there, if they didn't collapse from the taxing descent.

We found a gap in the bluffs of Boise Valley, where we turned down and succeeded in reaching the valley in safety although our road was very steep and stony and long.

—P. V. Crawford, August 6, 1851

BONNEVILLE POINT, SOUTHEAST OF BOISE, IDAHO*

A small adobe outpost of the Hudson's Bay Company stood on the eastern bank of the Snake River where it began its great sweep north to the Columbia River. Supplies and a ferry service were available there. At this point the river was wide, sluggish, and nearly uniform in depth, so fording it presented no problem to those who did not want to pay for the ferry.

Crossed Snake at Fort Boise, that world-renowned spot of one miserable block house all going to decay, this morning. Had no trouble in swimming the cattle.
—Charlotte Stearns Pengra,
August 13, 1853

CHAPTER FIVE

Oregon and Washington

After leaving the well-timbered crossing of the Snake River, the Oregon Trail again struck off through dry, treeless terrain. The emigrants who had chosen the southern route instead of crossing the Snake River at Three Island Crossing rejoined the main trail a few miles east of here.

~ . . . road led up through the hills . . . looked as if it had been intended for a public highway.

—Osborne Cross, August 30, 1849

KEENEY PASS, SOUTH OF VALE, OREGON*

The emigrants had kept uneasy company with the Snake River for most of the preceding three hundred miles. Now, at Farewell Bend, they would, in the words of one diarist, "bid hur a due forever." The next major river most of them would see was the mighty Columbia itself.

Came to Snake River for the last time. Here it runs between lofty and inaccessible mountains. So farewell Snake.

—Cecilia Emily McMillen Adams,
August 24, 1852

FAREWELL BEND STATE PARK, SOUTH OF HUNTINGTON, OREGON

ABOVE THE BURNT RIVER, NORTH OF LIME, OREGON

A very deep narrow wooded valley all along between high mountains . . . much dreaded.

—Samuel James, August 2, 1850

The overlanders entered the deep and confining Burnt River Canyon. Never before on the trail were they hemmed in by such precipitous, high hills. The bottom of the canyon, through which the river flowed, was so narrow that the wagons and cattle had to be carefully led over precarious trails worn into the steep hillsides.

142

Once again, the overlanders were forced to cross waterless, treeless, sagebrush-covered land. But this tract could be crossed in a day, and awaiting them was an ideal camping place in a broad valley laced with rivers and streams. At the end of the valley, though, was a narrow canyon, and from it they would have to climb up a large hill and descend into another valley.

143

A great bowl of a valley greeted the emigrants' eyes as they edged down Ladd Canyon Hill. The incline was covered with volcanic rock that was treacherously loose and slippery. The trees that stood conveniently at hand were put to good use as snubbing winches for lowering the wagons. Near the bottom, where the slope was not so steep, the pioneers could better appreciate the lovely valley before them.

Came in sight of the Grande Ronde, a beautiful level valley . . . but O the getting down to it over a long steep and stony hill is equal to any getting downstairs I ever saw, and I have seen some on this road.

—Cecilia Emily McMillen Adams,
September 2, 1852

Ladd Canyon Hill, Grande Ronde Valley, south of La Grande, Oregon

The Oregon Trail wended its way up and out of the Grande Ronde Valley to cross the heavily timbered, sharply sloping Blue Mountains. It was in the Blues that the emigrants saw the first of the great conifer forests of the Northwest. The size of the two-hundred-foot-tall trees and the dense forest growth astonished them. To those overlanders who had come from the eastern states, the familiar trees brought pangs of homesickness as they remembered the wooded hills they had left behind.

Worst hill to go down that we have found yet, long, steep and rocky. . . . Our road today has been mostly through lofty pines as fine as I ever saw.

—Cecilia Emily McMillen Adams, September 3, 1852

BLUE MOUNTAINS, NORTHWEST OF LA GRANDE, OREGON

The stream is about fifty feet wide, with clear water running over a nice pebbly bottom. The valley is very narrow, being only about sufficient for a wagon roadbed.

—P. V. Crawford, August 21, 1851

Once down the first steep slope of the Blue Mountains, the Oregon Trail crossed the flashing waters of the Grande Ronde River, which burbled through a pleasant valley.

Grand Ronde River Crossing, northwest of La Grande, Oregon

At Deadman Pass, the way was easy because the trail was nearly level, following a well-defined path through the trees.

OREGON TRAIL, DEADMAN PASS, BLUE MOUNTAINS*

From the heights of the western edge of the Blue Mountains, the pioneers could see the Cascade Mountains over 150 miles away—the only remaining barrier between them and their new home. The towering Mount Hood, Mount Saint Helens, and Mount Adams rose distinctly above the lower-lying, lesser mountains of the range.

From the brow of the mountain we had a fine view of the Cascade Range.

—Overton Johnson and William H. Winter, 1843

MOUNT ADAMS FROM DEADMAN PASS, SOUTHEAST OF PENDLETON, OREGON

The slow, rugged way over the Blue Mountains came to an end when the wagons went down the long slope of Emigrant Hill into the Umatilla River Valley, its vegetation by now a tawny autumn color.

At last came in sight of the valley, covered entirely with dry grass. Commenced the descent . . . very gradual. Said to be five miles downhill. Don't think it was much overrated.

—Cecilia Emily McMillen Adams, October 8, 1852

EMIGRANT HILL, EAST OF MISSION, OREGON*

Dr. Marcus Whitman and his wife, Narcissa, founded the Whitman Mission in 1836. She and another missionary's wife in the Whitman train were the first white women to cross the continent. The Oregon Trail passed some twenty miles south of the mission, but thousands of overlanders detoured to the place between 1843 and 1847. Dr. Whitman took care of the sick, provided supplies, and sometimes gave shelter to those who had started too late to get across the Cascades before winter set in.

On November 29, 1847, the Cayuse Indians attacked the mission. The Whitmans and twelve others were killed. All the mission buildings were destroyed and never rebuilt.

The buildings are of unburnt brick, and are neatly and comfortably furnished. The missionaries have a mill, and cultivate a small piece of ground.

—Overton Johnson and William H. Winter, 1843

Whitman Mission National Historic Site, west of Walla Walla, Washington

Had to camp at a mud hole spring call[ed] the Well Spring. Think it is a pretty sick one myself, at least we had to carry out about two wagonloads of mud before we could get water enough for cooking purposes.

—John Tully Kerns, September 10, 1852

In the empty, sere land west of the Umatilla River, Well Spring was the only source of water for miles, and it was barely drinkable.

UPPER WELL SPRING, WEST OF BUTLER JUNCTION, OREGON

After inching down steep, volcanic hills to the John Day River, the shallowness of the ford was welcome, but its cobblestone-like bottom made the crossing difficult. The gray, slippery rocks afforded no secure footing.

Dreadful hills and a bad rocky stream to cross.

—Samuel James, August 18, 1850

John Day River Crossing, southwest of Shutler, Oregon

The Willamette Valley seemed elusive and distant when the overlanders passed through this bleak, unfriendly country. Yet from here their destination was less than a hundred miles away.

Me think if this be Oregon it is not the place I started for.

—John Tully Kerns, September 1852

COLUMBIA PLATEAU, SOUTH OF BIGGS, OREGON

After reaching The Dalles, the emigrants had to choose between finishing their journey by the treacherous and expensive water passage down the Columbia River, or by a longer, somewhat less hazardous land route using the Barlow Road, which crossed the Cascade Mountains on the southern flank of Mount Hood.

The craft used for the harrowing voyage down the Columbia were either rafts, jerry-built boats of some sort, or dugout canoes. Most were inadequate to begin with and unstable when overloaded with people and their belongings. If the emigrants didn't sell their wagons at The Dalles, they lashed them onto log rafts that barely remained afloat with their heavy burdens. Livestock were herded along a precipitous trail on the cliffs that paralleled the river, through a forest so dense that in places it was dark as night.

The free-running Columbia plunged over waterfalls, through rapids, and coursed its way amid rock-strewn channels. As if this were not enough to plague the emigrants, gale-force winds frequently funneled down the deep, narrow gorge. Driven by the wind, boats were often forced onto the shore or, worse, wrecked on rocks; there were few places to make a safe landing. Progress often had to be halted for days until the winds abated.

COLUMBIA RIVER, NEAR NORTH BONNEVILLE, WASHINGTON

This is hard looking country, the roaring falls on one side, high rocky bluffs on the other, high peak of the Cascades in front.

—Maria Belshaw, September 19, 1853

MULTNOMAH FALLS, WEST OF CASCADE LOCKS, OREGON

FORT VANCOUVER NATIONAL HISTORIC SITE,
VANCOUVER, WASHINGTON

We landed at Fort Vancouver, forty miles below the Cascade Falls. The buildings occupied as stores, warehouses, shops, residences, etc., make quite a village. The ground back for half a mile is elevated several hundred feet above the river. It is set with grass, and makes a very pretty appearance.

—Overton Johnson and William H. Winter, 1843

Upon reaching the Hudson's Bay Company's Fort Vancouver, the hard part of the journey was over, and vestiges of civilization were a welcome sight to the weary pioneers. Events that were ordinary before they left home now evoked comment. One young lady said succinctly: "Ate on a table. Slept in a house." Another, savoring the food he was offered, wrote: "She gave me an apple and a piece of bread and butter. Maybe you think it wasn't good."

Dr. John McLoughlin, the fort's chief factor, was always willing to do everything within his power to help the emigrants get settled. He gave them not only advice, but also food, clothing, and other supplies they might need. Whether they could pay for what they received made no difference to this compassionate man. The Hudson's Bay Company disapproved of his beneficence toward the very people who were trying to displace England in the territory, so Dr. McLoughlin retired in 1846 and became an American citizen. For the next nine years, until his death in 1857, he continued to aid new settlers from his residence in Oregon City on the Willamette River.

FACTOR'S HOUSE, FORT VANCOUVER NATIONAL HISTORIC SITE, VANCOUVER, WASHINGTON

Those who wanted nothing to do with frail rafts and flimsy boats chose instead to go by way of the Barlow Road. They had another long pull onto the high, basalt plateau that rose sharply from The Dalles. Once on the heights, they were rewarded with a view of Mount Hood rising in magnificent solitude to the southwest.

Within a few miles, deep, narrow canyons began to branch from near the edge of the trail. Their steep sides were covered with a dense growth of oak. These were the first groves of deciduous trees the travelers had seen in nearly two thousand miles.

After one or two days' travel from The Dalles, the plateau suddenly opened onto the inviting Tygh Valley. Before the emigrants could reach it, however, they had to negotiate the infamous Tygh Valley grade—the only access to the valley was over the rounded shoulders of the high hills encircling it.

Descended one of the highest and longest hills we have saw yet in our travels.

—John Tully Kerns, September 22, 1852

TYGH VALLEY, OREGON*

Kentuckian Samuel K. Barlow was one of those who refused to pay the high fees demanded by the boat operators on the Columbia River. He felt sure there was a passage through the mountains. He found a way, or, rather, made one. He and the other men in his party literally hacked a road through the trees with a few dull, rusty tools. They piled up the felled timber at the edge of the road, atop the rotting, moss-covered deadfall of the forest floor.

At first, the Barlow Road was just wide enough for an oxen-pulled wagon to pass, and barely that. It wound its boulder-strewn way through dense forest, in the dank gloominess that pervades where sunlight never reaches the ground. On and upward the road tortuously went, with scarcely a break in the trees, to its summit of four thousand feet, on the slope of Mount Hood.

BARLOW ROAD NEAR BARLOW PASS, WEST OF WAMIC, OREGON*

Summit Meadow, a break in the seemingly interminable forest, was one of the few places where Mount Hood could be seen from the Barlow Road. But often the mountain peak wore a mantle of clouds and was obscured even from this close perspective, less than seven miles away. When they could see it, the emigrants admired the spectacle that nature had created, but they had other feelings about the campsite as they tried to make themselves comfortable for the night in the boggy, cold dampness of the meadow.

GROUND COVER IN SUMMIT MEADOW

Here we found good grass but the most terrible mud we had yet met with during the whole two thousand miles of travel.

—P. V. Crawford, September 14, 1851

Summit Meadow and Mount Hood, near Government Camp, Oregon

On the Barlow Road, the only way down from the heights of the Cascades was to descend Laurel Hill. Though now less than fifty miles from the end of the trail in Oregon City, the pioneers, long since bone weary, weak, debilitated, and often hungry because their food supply was nearly gone, had to confront this awesome slope.

Those who thought they had already seen the worst hill in the world changed their mind as soon as they got a look at the slope of Laurel Hill falling away at their feet. It was as though Providence had arranged one final test of the emigrants' worthiness before allowing them to settle in the promised land of Oregon.

When we came to Laurel Hill we viewed that descent in alarm. It looked as if we had come to the jumping off place. It seemed almost perpendicular and such a long descent.

—Adrietta Applegate Hixon, 1852

TOP OF LAUREL HILL, WEST OF GOVERNMENT CAMP, OREGON

The descent of Laurel Hill was made in two sections. The worst section was the first slope, with a vertical grade of 60 percent. A level bench, which offered the travelers a few minutes to catch their breath, led to the second slope, which was not quite so steep.

It was impossible to take the wagons down the hill by traversing it because they could not make sharp, right-angle turns. Instead they had to go over the brink and straight down the chute, which was covered with scree—loose, slippery, unstable rocks.

Usually the teams were unyoked and taken down a steep, narrow, winding trail. Some emigrants removed the wheels from their wagons and slid them down the incline. Another method was to lock the wheels, tie ropes to the wagon, snub the ropes around tree trunks, and pay them out, little by little, easing the wagon down. Often a large tree, as much as forty feet tall, was cut down and tied to the back of a wagon so its drag would serve as a brake. The discarded trees piled up at the bottom of the hill, making an effective stop for runaway wagons. But even all these precautions were not enough for one man, who said his wagon went down Laurel Hill "like shot off a shovel."

Negotiating Laurel Hill's precipitous drop was not the miserable travelers' only concern. The hungry oxen had to be continually watched to keep them from eating the leaves of the rhododendron—mistakenly called laurel—which are poisonous.

The locked wheels made a most dismal screeching sound that echoed back and forth through the woods.

—Adrietta Applegate Hixon, 1852

LAUREL HILL, WEST OF GOVERNMENT CAMP, OREGON

*Drove twelve miles,
crossing several small streams,
and winding our way over roots, stumps,
logs, brush, pole bridges, through mud holes,
and across marshy swales in the forest.*

—John Tully Kerns, September 28, 1852

BARLOW ROAD BELOW LAUREL HILL, WEST OF GOVERNMENT CAMP, OREGON*

Samuel Barlow charged a toll for use of the road he had constructed, and at first he located the tollgate at the road's western terminus. Having just traveled over the rough, primitive road, the emigrants were in no mood to pay for the privilege of having done so. It was not long before Barlow moved the collection point to the beginning of the road, east of the Cascades.

Once through the western tollgate, the pioneers were down the mountain and only forty miles from their destination, Oregon City, at the north end of the Willamette Valley. They had yet to cross the rugged, dizzyingly elevated Devils Backbone and ford the Sandy and Clackamas Rivers. At the beginning of the trail, the emigrants would have thought these major obstacles, but now the hardened travelers saw them as mere nuisances.

Almost through with a long and tiresome journey of almost six months. Taking all things into consideration had a pleasant trip.

—George N. Taylor, October 9, 1853

BARLOW ROAD TOLL GATE, RHODODENDRON, OREGON*

Relief and elation were coupled with near exhaustion after the emigrants finally traversed the last mile of the Oregon Trail. They had made it. Not without problems, and usually not without some tragedy, but they had done it. Now it was time to get on with the business of living.

I cannot realize that I am in a measure at my journey's end, with peace and plenty all around.

—Esther Belle Hanna, September 16, 1852

I now took off my blanket dress and put on my spick and span new dress and corded bonnet which I had carried safely on my saddle, and thus arrayed I staggered to the door. Mrs. Hatch caught me in her arms and her first words were, "Why dear woman, I supposed your clothing had been torn off your body long ago."

—Sarah J. Cummins, 1845

Went into a house to live again. The first one I had been in since we crossed the Missouri. H. nearly wild with joy. Did not want to camp out again.

—Lucia Loraine Williams, September 3, 1851

Friday, October 27. Arrived at Oregon City at the falls of the Willamette.

Saturday, October 28. Went to work.

—James W. Nesmith, 1843

185

Sites of Interest

Use the following listing to continue exploring the Oregon Trail. You can visit these sites in person or on the web.

National Park Service
www.nps.gov/fola/oregon.htm

MISSOURI
Jefferson Barracks Historic Park
Saint Louis, Missouri
314-544-5714
www.st-louiscountyparks.com

Jefferson National Expansion Memorial
Museum of Western Expansion
Saint Louis, Missouri
314-655-1700
www.nps.gov/jeff

National Frontier Trails Center
Independence, Missouri
816-325-7575
www.frontiertrailscenter.com

Mormon Visitors Center
Independence, Missouri
816-836-3466
www.lds.org/basicbeliefs/
placestovisit/1026.html

Kansas City Museum
Kansas City, Missouri
816-483-8300
www.kcmuseum.com

Saint Joseph Museum
Saint Joseph, Missouri
816-232-8471
www.stjosephmuseum.org

KANSAS
Fort Leavenworth Frontier Army Museum
Leavenworth, Kansas
913-684-3767
leav-www.army.mil/museum

**Hollenberg Pony Express
Station State Historic Site**
Hanover, Kansas
785-337-2635
www.kshs.org/places/hollenbg.htm

NEBRASKA
Rock Creek Station State Historic Park
Fairbury, Nebraska
402-729-5777
www.ngpc.state.ne.us/parks/rcstat.html

Fort Kearny State Historical Park
Kearney, Nebraska
308-865-5305
www.ngpc.state.ne.us/parks/ftkearny.html

Museum of Nebraska History
Lincoln, Nebraska
800-833-6747
www.nebraskahistory.org

Joslyn Art Museum
Omaha, Nebraska
402-342-3300
www.joslyn.org

The Mormon Trail Center at Historical Winter Quarters and Pioneer Cemetery
Omaha, Nebraska
402-453-9372
www.omaha.org/trails/trailctr.htm

Durham Western Heritage Museum
Omaha, Nebraska
402-444-5071
www.dwhm.org

Stuhr Museum of the Prairie Pioneer
Grand Island, Nebraska
308-385-5316
www.stuhrmuseum.org

Ash Hollow State Historical Park
Lewellen, Nebraska
308-778-5651
www.ngpc.state.ne.us/parks/hollow.html

Chimney Rock National Historic Site
Bayard, Nebraska
308-568-2581
www.nebraskahistory.org

Scotts Bluff National Monument
Gering, Nebraska
308-436-4340
www.nps.gov/scbl

WYOMING
Fort Laramie National Historic Site
Fort Laramie, Wyoming
307-837-2221
www.nps.gov/fola

Guernsey Visitors Center (for information on Register Cliff State Historic Site and Oregon Trail Ruts State Historic Site)
Guernsey, Wyoming
307-835-2715

Wyoming Pioneer Memorial Museum
Douglas, Wyoming
307-358-9288
www.wyshs.org/mus-wypioneer.htm

Douglas Area Chamber of Commerce
(for information on Ayres Natural Bridge)
Douglas, Wyoming
307-358-2950
www.jackalope.org

Casper Area Convention and Visitors Bureau
Casper, Wyoming
800-852-1889
www.casperwyoming.org/visitors

Independence Rock State Historic Site
Alcova, Wyoming
307-577-5150
http://commerce.state.wy.us/sphs/rock1.htm

South Pass City State Historic Site
South Pass City, Wyoming
307-332-3684
http://commerce.state.wy.us/sphs/south.htm

Fort Bridger State Historic Site
Fort Bridger, Wyoming
307-782-3842
http://commerce.state.wy.us/sphs/bridger.htm

IDAHO
Soda Springs Chamber of Commerce
Soda Springs, Idaho
208-547-4964
www.sodaspringsid.com

Fort Hall Replica
Pocatello, Idaho
208-234-1795
http://poky.net/forthall

Massacre Rocks State Park
American Falls, Idaho
208-548-2672
www.idahoparks.org/parks/massacre.html

Twin Falls Area Chamber of Commerce
(for information on Twin Falls
and Shoshone Falls)
Twin Falls, Idaho
800-255-8946
www.twinfallschamber.com

Buhl Chamber of Commerce
(for information on Thousand Springs)
Buhl, Idaho
208-543-6682
www.2chambers.com/buhl,_idaho.htm

Bruneau Dunes State Park
Bruneau, Idaho
208-366-7919
www.idahoparks.org/parks/bruneaudunes.html

Malad Gorge State Park
Bliss, Idaho
208-837-4505
www.idahoparks.org/parks/maladgorge.html

Three Island Crossing State Park
Glenns Ferry, Idaho
208-336-2394
www.idahoparks.org/parks/threeisland.html

Boise Convention and Visitors Bureau
(for information on Bonneville Point)
Boise, Idaho
800-635-5240
www.boise.org

OREGON
Farewell Bend State Park
Huntington, Oregon
541-869-2365
www.oregonstateparks.org/park_7.php

**National Historic Oregon Trail
Interpretive Center**
Baker City, Oregon
541-523-1843
www.or.blm.gov/NHOTIC/

**Oregon Trail Interpretive Park
at the Blue Mountain Crossing**
La Grande, Oregon
541-962-8589
www.fs.fed.us/r6/w-w/rog/
trails-lg/ortrail-th.htm

Columbia Gorge Discovery Center and
Wasco County Historical Museum
The Dalles, Oregon
541-296-860
www.gorgediscovery.org

Fort Dalles Museum
The Dalles, Oregon
541-296-4547
www.ohwy.com/or/f/fortdalm.htm

End of the Oregon Trail
Interpretive Center
Oregon City, Oregon
503-657-9336
www.endoftheoregontrail.org/index.html

John McLoughlin House
National Historic Site
Oregon City, Oregon
503-656-5146
www.endoftheoregontrail.org/mchouse.html

Oregon History Center
Portland, Oregon
503-222-1741
www.ohs.org

WASHINGTON
Columbia Gorge Interpretive Center
Stevenson, Washington
800-991-2338
www.columbiagorge.org

Beacon Rock State Park
Stevenson, Washington
509-427-8265
www.parks.wa.gov/alpha.asp
(Click on "Beacon Rock State Park")

Fort Vancouver National Historic Site
Vancouver, Washington
800-832-3599
www.nps.gov/fova

Bibliography

Adams, Cecilia Emily McMillen. Diary. MS. 1508. Oregon Historical Society Manuscript Library (here after cited as OHSML), Portland.

Allyn, Henry A. "A Record of Daily Events during a Trip from Fulton County, Illinois, across the Plains to the Willamette Valley, Oregon Territory in the Year 1853." MS. 1508. OHSML.

Alt, David D., and Donald W. Hyndman. *Roadside Geology of Oregon*. Missoula, Mont.: Mountain Press Publishing Company, 1981.

Anderson, William Wright. Diary. MS. 1508. OHSML.

Applegate, Jesse. "A Day With the Cow Column in 1843." *Oregon Historical Quarterly* (hereafter cited as *OHQ*) A (December 1900).

Applegate, Virginia Watson. "Barlow Road 1849." MS. 233. OHSML.

Atkin, James. Journal. MS. 1508. OHSML.

Bailey, Walter. "The Barlow Road." *OHQ* 13 (September 1912).

Barlow, William. "Reminiscences of Seventy Years." *OHQ* 13 (September 1912).

Beal, Josiah. Narrative, 1847. MS. 1508. OHSML.

Beckham, Dr. Stephen Dow. "The Barlow Road." *The Overland Journal* 2, no. 3 (Summer 1984).

Belshaw, Maria Parsons. Diary, 1853. *OHQ* 33 (December 1932).

Boardman, John. "The Overland Journey from Kansas to Oregon in 1843." *Utah Historical Society Quarterly* 2 (October 1929).

Boone, George L. "Sketch of 1848 Trip." MS. 1508. OHSML.

Bowman, Frank. Diary, 1844–1872. MS. 1491. OHSML.

Brown, John. Journal. MS. 2363. OHSML.

Bruff, J. Goldsborough. Diary, 1849. MS. 50, Yale Collection of Western Americana. Yale University Library, New Haven, Conn.

Buckingham, Harriet T. Diary. MS. 1156. OHSML.

Burnett, Peter H. Letters, 1844. *OHQ* 3 (March 1902).

Butler, Mrs. "1853 Diary of the Rogue River Valley." Ed. Oscar Osburn Winther and Rose Dodge. *OHQ* 41 (December 1940).

Carey, Charles H., ed. *Journals of Theodore Talbot*. Portland, Ore.: Metropolitan Press, 1931.

Carnahan, Mary Ellen Morrison. Recollections. MS. 1177. OHSML.

Castle, Gwen. "Belshaw Journey, Oregon Trail, 1853." *OHQ* 32 (September 1931).

Chambers, Margaret White. Reminiscences. MS. 1508. OHSML.

Churchill, Claire Warner, ed. "The Journey to Oregon: A Pioneer Girl's Diary." *OHQ* 29 (March 1928).

Clackamas County Historical Society and Wasco County Historical Society. "Barlow Road." Portland, Ore.: 1976. Brochure.

Clark, Thomas D. *Frontier America: The Story of the Westward Movement.* New York: Charles Scribner's Sons, 1959.

Condit, Philip. Diary, 1854. MS. 922. OHSML.

Condit, Sylvanus. Diary, 1854. MS. 923. OHSML.

Cooper, A. A. "Our Journey across the Plains from Missouri to Oregon, 1863." MS. 1508. OHSML.

Cornell, William. Diary. MS. 290. OHSML.

Cranston, Sarah Marsh. Journal. MS. 674. OHSML.

Crawford, P. V. "Journal of a Trip across the Plains, 1851." *OHQ* 25 (June 1924).

Cross, Osborne. *The March of the Mounted Riflemen.* Ed. Raymond W. Settle. Glendale, Calif.: Arthur H. Clark, 1940.

Cummins, Sarah J. Diary. MS. 1508. OHSML.

Davidson, Albert Franklin. Speech, and "Journal of Exploration in the Willamette Valley in Fall and Winter, 1845-46." MS. 386. OHSML.

Deady, Lucy Ann. "Crossing the Plains to Oregon in 1846." MS. 48. OHSML.

Dement, Russell C., and Ellis S. Dement. "After the Covered Wagons." Ed. E. R. Jackman. *OHQ* 63 (March 1962).

DeVoto, Bernard. *Across the Wide Missouri.* Boston: Houghton Mifflin, 1947.

Dowell, Benjamin Franklin. "Journal, Missouri to California, 1850." MS. 209. OHSML.

Dudley, Sarah Francis. "Trip across the Plains, 1852." MS. 1508. OHSML.

Duniway, Abigail Jane. "Overland Diary, 1852." MS. 432. OHSML.

Earl, Robert. Reminiscences, 1845. MS. 793. OHSML.

Eaton, Herbert. *The Overland Trail to California in 1852.* New York: G. P. Putnam's Sons, 1974.

Faris, John T. *On the Trail of the Pioneers.* New York: George H. Doran Company, 1920.

Field, James. "Crossing the Plains." MS. 520. OHSML.

Findley, William C. Diary. MS. 494. OHSML.

Fisher, Rev. Ezra. "Correspondence of Ezra Fisher." Ed. Sarah Fisher Henderson, Nellie E. Latourette, and Kenneth S. Latourette. *OHQ* 16 (December 1915).

Franzwa, Gregory M. *The Oregon Trail Revisited.* Tucson: Patrice Press, 1997.

———. *Maps of the Oregon Trail*. Tucson: Patrice Press, 1982.

Frémont, John Charles. *Expeditions of John Charles Frémont, 1843.* Ed. Donald Jackson and Mary Lee Spence. Urbana: University of Illinois Press, 1970.

Fry, John O. "A Trip across the Plains." MS. 427. OHSML.

Gaylord, Orange. "Overland Journey, 1853." MS. 726. OHSML.

Ghent, W. J. *The Road to Oregon: A Chronicle of the Great Emigrant Trail.* London, New York, and Toronto: Longmans, Green & Co., 1929.

Gibson, James. "Missouri to Oregon, 1847." MS. 141. OHSML.

Glenn, John G. Diary. MS. 284. OHSML.

Goltra, Mrs. E. J. Journal, 1853. MS. 1508. OHSML.

Hadley, Amelia. Diary. MS. 253. OHSML.

Haines, Aubrey L. *Historic Sites along the Oregon Trail.* Tucson: Patrice Press, 1981.

Hancock, Samuel. *Narrative, 1845.* Intro. by Arthur D. Howden-Smith. New York: R. M. McBride & Co., 1927.

Handsacker, Samuel. *Oregon Trail, 1853.* Eugene, Ore.: Lane County Pioneer Historical Society, 1965.

Hanna, Esther Belle. Diary, 1852. MS. 1508. OHSML.

Hanna, William. "Diary, Illinois to California, 1850." MS. 693. OHSML.

Harden, Absalom B. "Trail Diary, 1847." MS. 11. OHSML.

Harrison, J. M. "Account of Journey, 1846." MS. 1508. OHSML.

Harritt, Jesse H. Diary. MS. 947. OHSML.

Hastings, Loren B. Journal. MS. 660. OHSML.

Hayden, Mary Jane. "Pioneer Days." MS. 1508. OHSML.

Hemey, John Bunker. Diary, 1864. MS. 2605. OHSML.

Herren, John. "A Diary of 1845." MS. 224. OHSML.

Hewitt, Randall H. *Across the Plains and over the Divide.* New York: Argosy Antiquarian Ltd., 1964.

Hill, Sarah Almoran. "Journey to Oregon in 1843." MS. 1508. OHSML.

Hite, Joseph. Diary. MS. 1508. OHSML.

Hixon, Adrietta Applegate. "On to Oregon." MS. 1508. OHSML.

Hockett, William A. Diary. MS. 1036. OHSML.

Holmes, Kenneth L. *Covered Wagon Women.* Vols. 1–3. Glendale, Calif.: Arthur H. Clark, 1983.

Hooker, William Francis. *The Prairie Schooner.* Chicago: Saul Brothers, 1918.

Howell, John Ewing. Journal, 1845. MS. 659. OHSML.

Hunt, G. W. "To Oregon by Ox Team, 1847." MS. 1508. OHSML.

Hunt, Nancy A. "By Ox-Team to California." MS. 1508. OHSML.

Idaho Historical Society, Bicentennial Commission. *Route of the Oregon Trail in Idaho.* Boise: Idaho Historical Society: 1974.

James, Samuel. "Trip from Iowa to Oregon." MS. 1508. OHSML.

Johnson, Overton, and William H. Winter. "Migration of 1843." *OHQ* 7 (March 1906).

Kahler, William. Journal, 1852. MS. 277, Yale Collection of Western Americana. Yale University Library, New Haven, Conn.

Kerns, John Tully. Diary, 1852. MS. 1508. OHSML.

Ketcham, Rebecca. "From Ithaca to Clatsop Plains: Miss Ketcham's Journal of Travels." *OHQ* 42 (September 1961 and December 1961).

Lee, Anna Green. Diary. MS. 283. OHSML.

Lockley, Fred, ed. "Reminiscences of James E. R. Harrell." *OHQ* 24 (June 1923).

———, ed. "Recollections of Benjamin Franklin Bonney." *OHQ* 24 (March 1923).

Long, Mary Jane. "Crossing the Plains in the Year of 1852 with Ox Teams." MS. 1508. OHSML.

Longmire, James. Diary. MS. 1004. OHSML.

Longworth, Basil N. *Diary, 1853.* Denver: D. E. Harrington, 1927.

Martin, Charles W. "The Alcove Spring." *Overland Journal* 2, no. 1 (Winter 1984).

Mattes, Merrill J. *The Great Platte River Road.* Lincoln: Nebraska State Historical Society, 1969.

McCall, A. J. "The Great California Trail in 1849." (From the *Steuben Courier,* Steuben, New York, 1882.) MS. 1508. OHSML.

McClung, James S. Diary, 1862. MS. 1508. OHSML.

McClure, Andrew S. Diary. MS. 732B. OHSML.

McDannald, David Walker. Diary. MS. 1508. OHSML.

McKaig, Silas. Diary, 1852. MS. 151. OHSML.

McKean, Samuel Terry. "Reminiscences, 1847." MS. 483. OHSML.

McNary, Lawrence A. "Route of the Meek Cutoff, 1845." *OHQ* 35 (March 1934).

Meeker, Ezra. *The Ox Team, or the Old Oregon Trail.* Omaha: Ezra Meeker, 1907.

Miller, James D. "Early Oregon Scenes: A Pioneer Narrative." *OHQ* 31 (March 1930).

Minto, Hon. John. "Reminiscences of a Pioneer of 1844." *OHQ* 2 (June 1901).

Moreland, Rev. Jesse. "Journey of 1852." MS. 1508. OHSML.

Morfitt, William. "Memories of '47." MS. 1508. OHSML.

Munger, Asahel, and wife. "Diary, 1839." *OHQ* 8 (December 1907).

Musil, Faye. "Overland Forts." *Nebraskaland* 59, no. 13 (September 1981).

Myres, Sandra L. *Ho for California.* San Marino, Calif.: Henry E. Huntington Library and Art Gallery, 1980.

National Geographic Society. "Trails West." Washington, D.C., 1979.

Nebraska Game and Parks Commission. "The Oregon Trail." Pamphlet.

Nesmith, James W. "Diary of the Emigration of 1843." *OHQ* 7 (December 1906).

Newby, William T. "Diary of the Emigration." *OHQ* 40 (September 1939).

Oakly, Obadiah. "Expedition to Oregon, 1842." MS. 1508. OHSML.

Pabian, Roger K., and James B. Swinehart II. *Geologic History of Scotts Bluff National Monument.* Lincoln: Conservation and Survey Division, Institute of Agriculture and Natural Resources, University of Nebraska, 1979.

Paden, Irene D. *The Wake of the Prairie Schooner.* Carbondale and Edwardsville: Southern Illinois University Press, 1970.

Palmer, Harriet Scott. "Crossing over the Great Plains by Ox Wagons, 1852." MS. 1508. OHSML.

Palmer, Joel. "Journal of Travels over the Rocky Mountains 1845-1846." In *Early Western Travels.* Vol. 30. Ed. Reuben Gold Thwaites. Cleveland: Arthur H. Clark, 1906.

Parker, Samuel. Diary, 1845. MS. 1508. OHSML.

Parker, Rev. Samuel. *Journal of an Exploring Tour beyond the Rocky Mountains.* Ithaca, NY: Mack, Andrus & Woodruff, 1842.

Parkman, Francis. *The Oregon Trail.* Garden City, NY: Doubleday & Co., 1946.

Patterson, Laura A. Hawn. "Recollections, 1843." MS. 381. OHSML.

Pattison, William. Diary. MS. 1072. OHSML.

Pease, David Egbert. Diary, 1849. MS. 60. OHSML.

Pengra, Charlotte Stearns. Diary, 1853. Lane County Pioneer Historical Society, Eugene, Oregon.

Pfouts, Paris Swazey. Diary. MS. 297. OHSML.

Pringle, Catherine Sager. "Recollections." MS. 1194-1. OHSML.

Pringle, Virgil. Diary. MS. 1194. OHSML.

Raynor, James. Diary. MS. 1508. OHSML.

Reed, Henry E. "Lovejoy's Pioneer Narrative." *OHQ* 31 (September 1930).

Reid, John Phillip. "Replenishing the Elephant." *OHQ* 79 (Spring 1978).

Renshaw, Robert Harvey. Diary. MS. 418. OHSML.

Robe, Rev. Robert. Diary, 1851. MS. 1163. OHSML.

Rogers, Martha Ellen. "Reminiscences." MS. 697. OHSML.

Ruddell, W. H. "Trip across the Plains, 1851." MS. 1508. OHSML.

Sage, Rufus B. *Rufus B. Sage, His Letters and Papers 1836–1847 and Scenes in the Rocky Mountains.* Vols. 4 and 5 of *The Far West and the Rockies Historical Series 1820–1875.* Ed. LeRoy R. Hafen and Ann W. Hafen. Glendale, Calif.: Arthur H. Clark, 1956.

Sargent, Elisha Nelson. Diary. MS. 813. OHSML.

Saunders, Delila Berintha. Diary, 1866. MS. 1508. OHSML.

Scott, Charlton. Diary, 1862. MS. 1054B. OHSML.

Smith, Elizabeth Dixon. Diary. MS. 641. OHSML.

Spaulding, Kenneth A., ed. *On the Old Oregon Trail: Robert Stuart's Journey of Discovery.* Norman: University of Oklahoma Press, 1953.

Spencer, John B. Diary, 1852. MS. 1508. OHSML.

Starbuck, Edith. *Crossing the Plains.* Nashville: Southern Publishing Association, 1927.

Starr, J. R. "Diary from Iowa to Idaho, 1850." MS. 2473. OHSML.

Stevens, Charles. "Letters of Charles Stevens, 1852." *OHQ* 37 (June 1936).

Stewart, George R. *The California Trail.* Lincoln: University of Nebraska Press, 1962.

Strachan, John. "Blazing the Millan Trail." MS. 1508. OHSML.

Sutton, Sarah. Diary. MS. 2280. OHSML.

Taylor, George N. Diary. MS. 1508. OHSML.

Taylor, John S. Diary, 1854. MS. 17. OHSML.

Taylor, S. H. "Oregon Bound: Letters to the Watertown Chronicle, Watertown, Wisconsin." *OHQ* 22 (June 1921).

Thomson, Origen. Diary. MS. 1508. OHSML.

Unruh, John D., Jr. *The Plains Across.* Urbana: University of Illinois Press, 1982.

Vanbuskirk, William. Diary, 1852. MS. 881. OHSML.

Ward, D. B. "Across the Plains in 1853." MS. 1508. OHSML.

Ware, Joseph, E. *The Emigrant's Guide to California.* Princeton, NJ: Princeton University Press, 1932.

Warren, Daniel Knight. "Reminiscences." *OHQ* 3 (September 1902).

West, Calvin B. Journal and Letters, 1853. MS. 692. OHSML.

West, George Miller. "Crossing the Plains." MS. 1508. OHSML.

Wigle, Abraham J. "Account of Overland Journey, 1852." MS. 587. OHSML.

Williams, Veleria A. Journal. MS. 1508. OHSML.

Wood, Elizabeth. "Journal of a Trip to Oregon, 1851." *OHQ* 27 (March 1926).

Wood, Tallmadge B. "Letter." *OHQ* 3 (March 1902).

Woodcock, William C. Diary. MS. 982. OHSML.

Wyeth, John B., and John Kirk Townsend. *The Overland Journey of John B. Wyeth and John Kirk Townsend.* Fairfield, Wash.: Ye Galleon Press, 1970.

Young, John Quincy Adams. Diary. MS. 187. OHSML.

Zieber, John S. "Journal, Peoria, Illinois, to Oregon City, 1851." MS. 1508. OHSML.

Index

About the Authors

Husband and wife **Bill and Jan Moeller** are professional photographers and authors. Since 1982 they have traveled full-time in their RV to photograph historical sites around the United States. Having their home with them allows the Moellers to stay in an area as long as necessary to take pictures and do research for their unique photographic history books.

Before embarking on their land-based ventures, the Moellers lived aboard a sailboat for twelve years, touring the Atlantic Coast. In addition to their photo histories, the authors have published books and articles on sailing and RVing. Other Moeller photographic history books published by Mountain Press include *Chief Joseph and the Nez Perces: A Photographic History* (ISBN 0-87842-319-2), *Lewis & Clark: A Photographic Journey* (ISBN 0-87842-405-9), and *Crazy Horse: A Photographic Biography* (ISBN 0-87842-424-5).

Other books by Bill and Jan Moeller:

Crazy Horse: A Photographic Biography
Lewis & Clark: A Photographic Journey
*Chief Joseph and the Nez Perces:
    A Photographic History*
*Custer, His Life, His Adventures:
    A Photographic Biography*

RVing Alaska by Land and Sea
*A Complete Guide to Full-time RVing:
    Life on the Open Road*
RVing Basics
RV Electrical Systems

*The Intracoastal Waterway:
    A Cockpit Cruising Handbook*
*Living Aboard:
    The Cruising Sailboat as a Home*

We encourage you to patronize your local bookstore. Most stores will order any title that they do not stock. You may also order directly from Mountain Press using the order form provided below or by calling our toll-free number and using your MasterCard, VISA, American Express, or Discover. We will gladly send you a complete catalog upon request.

Some other titles of interest:

_____*The Oregon Trail: A Photographic Journey* $18.00/paper

_____*Crazy Horse: A Photographic Biography* $20.00/paper

_____*Lewis & Clark: A Photographic Journey* $18.00/paper

_____*Sacagawea's Son: The Life of Jean Baptiste Charbonneau* $10.00/paper (for readers 10 and up)

_____*Stories of Young Pioneers: In Their Own Words* $14.00/paper (for readers 10 and up)

_____*The Arikara War: The First Plains Indian War, 1823* $18.00/paper $30.00/cloth

_____*The Journals of Patrick Gass:*
       Member of the Lewis and Clark Expedition $20.00/paper $36.00/cloth

_____*Chief Joseph and the Nez Perces: A Photographic History* $15.00/paper

_____*Lakota Noon: The Indian Narrative of Custer's Defeat* $18.00/paper $36.00/cloth

_____*Children of the Fur Trade:*
       Forgotten Métis of the Pacific Northwest $15.00/paper

_____*The Piikani Blackfeet: A Culture Under Siege* $18.00/paper $30.00/cloth

_____*William Henry Jackson: Framing the Frontier* $22.00/paper $36.00/cloth

Please include $3.00 per order to cover shipping and handling.

Send the books marked above. I enclose $_____

Name _____

Address _____

City/State/Zip _____

☐ Payment enclosed (check or money order in U.S. funds)

Bill my: ☐ VISA ☐ MasterCard ☐ American Express ☐ Discover   Expiration Date:_____

Card No._____

Signature_____

MOUNTAIN PRESS PUBLISHING COMPANY
P.O. Box 2399 • Missoula, MT 59806 • fax: 406-728-1635
Order Toll Free 1-800-234-5308 • Have your credit card ready.
e-mail: mtnpress@montana.com • website: www.mountainpresspublish.com